How the World Ends

John Stanton

DEDICATION

Damien, Aaron, Jill, Scylla, Theresa

LoRicco, Clarke, DeRosa, Cal, Lieneck,
Marty, Fraser, Driesbaugh, Philpott, Nina,
LTG Skibbie, MG Eicher, RADM Lewis, MG McInereny,
Sandra Erwin, Bob Williams, Vin, Bron, Blauvelt, Lempke,
Joan Marley, Ron Files, Dan Murphy

Jeffrey St. Clair, Counterpunch
Dmitry Sudakov, Pravda Report
Angie, Dissident Voice
Jeff Tedrich, Smirking Chimp
Bev, Intrepid Report
Joseph, Seoul Times
John Young & Deborah Natsios, Cryptome
Editor, Countercurrents
Editor, Sri Lanka Guardian
Editors, Scoop—New Zealand

CONTENTS

A collection of essays published in late 2020 to June 2021.

ACKNOWLEDGMENTS

"It is the writer's duty to tell the terrible truth and it is the reader's civic duty to learn this truth."

Vasily Grossman, The Road

Books by Vasily Grossman that should be required reading for every student and adult in the United States of America.

Life and Fate (sequel to Stalingrad)
Stalingrad
Everything Flows

CHAPTER 1: HOW THE WORLD ENDS

I'm writing this letter to myself. I need to talk to someone, even it is only my own self. I need to believe that what happened was real.

All that I know of the past was learned by word-of-mouth histories from those who came before me and those few historians who remain now. Some matters I know directly. We don't talk much anymore to each other because it takes too much physical effort. It has been tiring to write this letter by the dim light available to me either in or outdoors, day or night. But it helps to distract me from the situation everyone is in.

I was part of the BMR or the Baltimore Metro Resistance. I was part of the BMR when I was young and I guess I still am a member now. My parents migrated to Baltimore from Virginia. They are gone now, killed in fighting by bullet, blade, bomb, artillery or missile. That's what I was told. I often wish now that I would have died with them, such are the circumstances these days.

There were other resistance groups in the former United States of America that I know of: Los Angeles, Houston, New Orleans, Saint Louis, Chicago, Detroit, Boston, New York City, Philadelphia, Charlotte (North Carolina) and Miami. Millions flocked to these locations in hopes of defending themselves from the brutal federal and state militaries; para-military security forces and mercenaries, and local police.

When I was very young, I became a courier in the BMR transporting everything from letters, food, ammunition, tools, medicine, water. I eventually became a competent, adaptable fighter with about an average talent for writing. There were so many thousands of us that were BMR fighters but only about 100 of us at any one time had the responsibility to compose three page letters that would serve as a narrative of the day or night's activity. The letters included stories of combat, the details of terrain, retreat or advance, stalemates and casualties, poems, puzzles, trivia, anything that could be read for a few moments of escape. Once composed the many letters written by all of us went into a zip lock plastic bag, and circulated throughout our metro area for reading.

War

War does funny things, I suppose, like bring people together or tearing them apart or both. In tearing apart the United States, the government, clearly not intending to do so, brought people together, at least in our case. Our BMR was made up of black, white, latino, asian, and mixed race fighters, young and old, LGBTQ, anyone who accepted our cause. History, race, ethnicity or class no longer mattered to any of us. Sure, their were leaders and order necessary for operations, everyone below a leader was trained in how and when to fight and with what. Tactics and strategy did not belong to an elite particularly since no one could afford to be located at a central command post.

The only reference points in time I have for a starting point for the emergence of the resistance groups, or I suppose city-states, is 2020 to 2045. Beyond that, I don't know whether it is now late in the 21 St Century or early in 22 second Century. Our oral historians told us that, at least in the then United States, martial law was declared during those years and the US Constitution and Bill of Rights were suspended. Government pensions, medical benefits, food assistance, environmental protections and every form of civilian aid were suspended apparently in about 2025 by presidential order. Elections were also suspended with the president appointing those who he thought should represent the people. Tribunals took the place of courts. A few other presidents came and went, I was told, but the die was cast: the allure of power was too much to for anyone to care about the general populace.

These were frantic times in the BMR as everyone knew an attack by government forces was imminent. But with the number of metro areas offering refuge and armed resistance, plus the ongoing wars the government was waging overseas, there would have to be careful planning by the enemy military leaders. Our strategists and tacticians reminded us that high ranking government military commanders were plodding, conventional thinkers bound up in the false promises of technology.

I learned that during the initial setup of the BMR, major food and clothing chains, drug stores, camping and fishing outlets, boats docked of any type, fuel from gas stations, water sources, weapons of all types from gun shops and ammunition all took part in emptying their shelves and stocking all the goods at various hardened sites in the BMR. Bank vaults, below ground parking garages and wherever there was a below ground facility were stocked. Prepositioned stocks of weapons, ammo and food were stored outside the Baltimore City limits. Shipping containers loaded with canned goods or plastic water bottles were submerged in the Baltimore harbor.

Tunnel construction began in earnest, tiered defenses were setup for BMR's inner, outer and suburban areas. Choke points were set that would funnel attackers into kill zones. Booby traps, crude land-mines and even crossbows were used during the fight. Bicycles and skate boards were put to good use since fuel was severely rationed. Methods of communication had to be devised that would not emit heat because they would be detected by electronic warfare packages on enemy aircraft. We had to devise a low flying drone defense and we had to find a way to hide critical weapons and stores from satellites. Again, we lucked out because a lot of satellite and drone time was allocated by the government forces to their overseas conflicts.

Advantages

We had the good fortune to have in the BMR Johns Hopkins medical and research personnel on our side along with most of the air and space staff moving in with us from Goddard space flight center not far away. Many from nearby Fort Meade and some from the former National Security Agency joined us. I am not sure of the functions of many of those people but I know that doctors, technologists, space researchers and weapons developers were among them. We were able to develop our own drones that were used for reconnaissance.

I have heard that nearly 40 percent of those forces joined the resistance bringing with them weapons, munitions, vehicles and, more importantly, training. I learned too that a some Virginia Class Submarines, three strategic ballistic missile nuke submarines, a handful of AEGIS warships, and even one Carrier Strike Group joined the resistance too.

Of those, two Virginia Class attack submarines joined the BMR along with two AEGIS warships. Initially, no one in the BMR was sure what to do with this firepower but it didn't take long for the technologists and military personnel that came ashore to suggest good use of the Navy vessels. The one SSBN that was aligned with the BMR may have served as a deterrent to the government nuking us. But it and one of the two Virginia attack class subs would have to take to the deep ocean to be effective. I did not learn of their fate. We were not nuked, I know that.

The other attack submarine that stayed with us had a nuclear power source. I don't understand how they did it (though we did have some pretty smart people in our camp) but they were able to move the nuclear power source to a facility deep within the BMR. I guess the idea was to use it to power a BMR of the future. I'm not sure what came of that effort though in the end it didn't matter.

The Virginia attack sub arrived to us loaded with cruise missiles and a couple of Navy SEAL units. The SEALS would push back an attack by other Navy SEALS dispatched by submersible from pro-government submarines to infiltrate and terrorize the BMR. They were essential to our defense and raiding/scouting efforts.

Cruise missiles were fired from our Virginia attack sub and I think they found their way to artillery and tank emplacements that initially surrounded us. The AEGIS warships managed to fend off some aircraft and missile attacks but ultimately succumbed to anti-ship missiles homing in on their heat signatures. The sub was eventually sunk by torpedo, I think.

Lucky

We figured we had a fighting chance against our opponents but make no mistake: it was because events were taking place outside the United States that might make our struggle successful. It is one thing to quell an internal rebellion, quite another to succeed against 100 million resistance fighters tucked away in metro areas while trying to win wars in foreign lands, on and below the world's oceans, and in space. We figured that our opponents would eventually run short of fuel and munitions with so many to fight and we, luckily, were right.

Still, like all the other resistance groups around in the former United States and around the world , we lost thousands and thousands during the relentless barrages from air, sea and land. We started out poorly in defending the BMR on the ground but after fits and starts managed to push back our enemies. We learned that the Miami, Florida and Charlotte. North Carolina BMRs were defeated. Both Florida and North Carolina had a heavy government military presence and even with the help of those in the military that came to the aid of the resistance it wasn't enough.

We celebrated the cessation of fighting for a short time. We all were skeptical that it was really over but our scouting parties found abandoned tanks, vehicles, artillery pieces and a lot of dead and decaying bodies. The peace was short lived. Then nukes came. And then the planet rebelled.

During some short time period, some fateful decisions were made by the former United States, Russia, Pakistan, India and China.

Who knows the sequence but the end result was horrifying. I guess the first thing to say was that China decided that US Pacific fleet forces, the three Carrier Strike Groups there, were vulnerable. China decided to take on those forces with their conventional forces and suffered badly. The Chinese surface, subsurface and air forces were largely destroyed. Given that hundreds of millions of their own people were fighting their Peoples Liberation Army within their own borders the vaunted advantage of PLA ground forces vanished. With their naval forces destroyed by the United States and Pacific allies, they decided to launch nuclear weapons at Japan, Okinawa, Guam and Taiwan where the US fleet had a presence. The same weapons were launched at the three carrier groups in the China area of operations with the result being the elimination of US forces.

At the same time. Russia decided that the time was ripe for moving further into Ukraine, the Baltic's and Europe, into a barely armed Germany. Meager NATO forces supported by sacrificial US support units were no match for the Russians. Seeing defeat, the US launched scores of tactical nukes to stop the onslaught. At the same times, India and Pakistan decided to settle their scores by launching their stock of nukes at each other. Nuclear warheads flew between those two countries and around the globe. We learned that Newport News, San Diego, sub bases on the East and west coasts of the United States were destroyed by nukes. Washington, DC,

Houston and New Orleans were also eliminated. Ground based missiles anywhere in the world, in our case in the Northwest, were cratered by nukes turning those places into radioactive no go zones.

The Nukes Time ended. Our skies were psychedelic with colors that defied sense. Orange, gray, blue, yellow, black colors would appear each day. It was getting cold as the sun seemed to fade into the distance. Our Geiger counters registered high but tolerable radiation. But many of us started feeling sick.

We learned, thanks to our telecommunications, internet and satellite technicians that the scene was the same all over the planet. Populations of the former United States, Russia, China, India, Pakistan Europe, Brazil, Malaysia, Mexico Indonesia, the African nations, were all now displaced moving by sea or land in hopes of surviving somewhere.

After the Nuke Time there was another calm period. Many of us were worried about this. We had all forgotten about Climate Change and planetary disturbances.

Earth Revolts

I remember one day waking up in the BMR thinking that the Earth had fallen away under me. I learned that the West Coast earthquake had finally come putting Los Angeles and the West Coast of the United States into the Pacific ocean. The volcano that was said to be dormant in the Pacific northwest exploded sending soot and tremors throughout the former United States. It was undeniable that the Earth said Enough! There were earthquakes and subsequent Tsunami's everywhere. Volcanic eruptions around the Earth were so severe that the sky turned black.

Snowflakes made of ash fell from the sky. Respiratory distress was the norm. People coughed so hard that they vomited blood.

Probably the worst image of the times was picked up by a couple of our drones roaming over Ocean City, Maryland. Marine life started to appear on the beaches dead or dying. Thousands of people mauled each other and the dead, beached creatures for something to eat. The video was awful particularly since we knew that anyone eating the toxic meat from the oceans would have convulsions and vomiting with 24 hours and would die. The worst thing we saw from these video feeds was that people slaughtered each other for what they thought was good food.

All the coastal cities in the world are gone, sunk into the oceans. The oceans have turned into some viscous polluted mass. The seas and vicious weather pursue us up into the high ground or wherever we go.

I am ending this letter. I will drink a pint of vodka, take many opioids and go into the black. But before that, I will put this letter into the zip lock bag and bury it somewhere.

****

Sir.

Yes, what is it.

Our sentient droids scattered around and above this planet have uploaded our data for analyses into the primary ship.

Good.

Make sure that all the sentient programming on this planet is upload back into the bio machinery There is much to analyze.

Of course, sir.

Sir, one of our archeo devices has come across what appears to be a first hand account of the demise of this planet.

Good, construct it, translate it and send it to me.

Yes.

Are you ok ,sir?

Yes, this narrative is very sad, moving even. Well, put this in the archives with the other data retrieved from this planet.

Again, do not leave any of our sentient programs in this place. Send out warning satellites outside the ring of debris that surrounds this planet. Send out a warning using universal Planck communications that this place is toxic.

Let us move out of this solar system.

——

CHAPTER 2: GOODBYE DR. SEUSS

"Since August 20, the young Red Guards of Peking, detachments of students,have taken to the streets. With the revolutionary rebel spirit of the proletariat, they have launched a furious offensive to sweep away reactionary, decadent bourgeois and feudal influences, and all old ideas, culture, customs and habits. This mounting revolutionary storm is sweeping the cities of the entire nation.Red Guards and revolutionary students and teachers in Lhasa have proposed to change the names of places, streets and houses which are tainted with feudal serfdom and superstition. They also propose that literary and art groups forbid the performance of operas and plays which reek of imperialism and feudalism. The waterfront of the Whangpoo River in Shanghai was, until the liberation, the centre of imperialist plunder of the Chinese people. The buildings here have still carried many reminders of the imperialists and here the Red Guards and revolutionary workers and staff have gone in for revolutionizing in a big way. They have taken down all the imperialist signs from walls and removed the bronze lions outside one of the big buildings."

– Peking ("Beijing") Review, 1966

PREFACE: My grandson is a mix of Amazonian Indian, Brazilian, Portuguese, Indian (India), Trinidadian and Irish. Certainly, in all the cultures his genes arise from, there is current and historical racism, slavery, discrimination, class issues and so on. Does he bear any responsibility for all the sins of the past other than to be consciously aware of it all and be sensitive to how it affects the present (will influence his present one day)? The grandkid looks non-white, and I know this means, unfortunately, in parts of the United States and certain regions of the world, he may be mocked and subjected to racism/discrimination. Does this mean I know what it is like not to be White and have had a revelation thanks to the probabilities that my grandson appears as a non-White? No. It just means chance and evolution were at work. Perhaps the world will reboot over the next 17 years. I wrote a bit about this subject in 2015 which can be read here: *White and Guilty of the Crime of History? I'm not Going to the Reeducation Camp* (dissidentvoice.org).

And I agree with Teju Cole's point about the White Savior Industrial Complex theory. That starts with protesting against tortuous US foreign policy that makes it worse for nations on the African Continent.

"Let us begin our activism right here: with the money-driven villainy at the heart of American foreign policy. To do this would be to give up the illusion that the sentimental need [of White people] to "make a difference" trumps all other considerations. What innocent heroes don't always understand is that they play a useful role for people who have much more cynical motives. The White Savior Industrial Complex is a valve for releasing the unbearable pressures that build in a system built on pillage."

Cole refers to Haiti and Nigeria, two countries that have borne the brunt of the American government's harshness. You could list most central American countries in that category too, including Venezuela.

So Long, Doctor Seuss of Dartmouth, You Did it to Yourself

No more Dr. Seuss's Sleep Book before bedtime, I guess. I once read the book myself in bed–as the instructions at the beginning of the book required ("this book is to be read in bed")–and I used to read it to my son. I still have the book and, I'll admit it, I look at it now and then. I still am fascinated by the Biffer-Baum Birds, the

Oft Aloft and I imagine what it might be like to be able to sleep in the Bed of the Jed, "The softest of beds in the world it is said." It still makes me sleepy.

And then there is the Cat in the Hat Comes Back. I read that book often myself and then, like Dr. Seuss's Sleep Book, I read that to my son too. I used the book to explain to my young one some of the intricacies of particle physics. You could not see VaVoom but you could see the results of its presence: The ink disappeared and so particle collisions, interactions must have taken place.

Anyway, those were the only two Dr. Seuss books I really favored. The rest were too preachy for me. Little did I realize that racialist undertones permeated many of the books and, alas, I was not politically or culturally attuned, like millions of others in the United States and around the globe, to the dismal facts set forth in a study by Ramon Stephens and Katie Ishizuka titled the Cat is Out of the Bag: Orientalism, Anti-Blackness and White Supremacy in Dr. Seuss' Children's Books. Their study has garnered 163,626 downloads and has had the positive effect of causing the publisher's of Dr. Seuss's books to stop pushing out the titles with the most offending cartoons.

Stephens and Ishizuka also noted that a mere 2 percent of Dr. Seuss's characters were not White, or appeared to be non-White. "In the fifty Dr. Seuss children's books, 2240 human characters are identified. Of the 2240, there are 45 characters of color representing 2% of the total number of human characters."

That small act of atonement by Seuss's publishing house will not matter though. Ultimately, Dr. Seuss's (Ted Geisel) titles will be banned by public and in-school libraries. As a children's book collection, they will become oddities used for further studies by enterprising critical literary and racial theorists for further analysis. The same fate awaits thousands of titles authored by "Whites" to include novels, cinema titles, cartoons, and corporate products displaying implied racial insensitivity.

Personally, I'm fine with exposes like that of Stephens and Ishizuka as long as they are not in-your-face, vengeful, punitive efforts at dumping on those in the 21st Century who had no earthly influence on the events of world history before 600 to the present. Racism (to include discrimination against LGBTQ+, in group versus out group, etc.), sadly, is endemic to the human species. We may rid ourselves of this maddening scourge probably around the same time as we eliminate nuclear weapons.Or, perhaps, Climate Change will get us all first.

Stay in Your Whatever Lane

Beyond correcting racial, discriminatory narratives, the core issue in these matters seems to me to be, To what extreme will cultural erasure go? Will Chairman Mao's or the Red Guards model be adopted here in the United States or elsewhere? At what point does racial and cultural awareness turn into a vindictive purge against all things Whiteness or against those other colors, religions that oppressed the weary? Does an erasure movement become regressive, anti-free speech and inhibit creativity? How far back in history does this dig travel? Who will be the inquisitors, guardians overseeing what clearly is a purge, a reeducation campaign? Should White people be eliminated? At what point does racism reverse to Black on White, Hispanic on Black, and so on. You get the idea.

People in the United States obviously would not be the first to pull down the statues of those who engaged in enslaving people and looked the other way while many of the oppressed were hanged/murdered simply because of their skin color and class position in society. Statues of Stalin, Lenin, and Saddam Hussein were all brought down by citizens, mainly the young and middle class, in the former Soviet Union and the "old" Iraq, who lived under tyrannical rule and were hustled off to gulags or persecuted because of culture-religion or class position. The conquering Americans got into that culture changing gig during the second invasion of Iraq pointing to an interesting fact about human history: the conquerors usually determine the rules and the historical narratives. That changes over time as the conquered assimilate the conquerors or eventually overtake them by revolution. And so the cycle repeats itself. At some point in the future, the same will happen to the United States.

So just how should an author of novels, a screenwriter or a children's storyteller go about their craft these days? Perhaps characters should be created and colored representing the demographics of the country in which the creative person is a citizen. Take, for example, a person who lives in the United States decides one day to write an epic novel of love, hate and redemption. That work would have the percentage of its characters mirror the Census.Gov demographics. To wit, the novel should contain: White, 60.1 to 76.3; Hispanic or Latino, 18.5%; Black, 13.4%; Asian, 5.9%; Two or more races, 2.8%; American Indian/Alaska Native, 1.3% and Native Hawaiian/Pacific Islander, 0.2%. And approximately 4% identify as LGBTQ+

These percentages reflect the population of the United States and so shouldn't authors, scriptwriters, filmmakers make sure they've included the exact percentages? Would that be acceptable to critical race, literary theory? I don't think so.

There is another issue here: Authors, scriptwriters, and filmmakers must adhere to the "no lane change rule;" that is, a White author can't have characters that are Black, Hispanic/Latino or Asian because he/she/person can't get into that person's color or look invalidating the character's credibility. On the other hand, Blacks, Hispanic/Latino or Asian authors can't create White characters, the same way that Asians can't have characters who are Black, and so it goes.

The next matter of concern, let's say for an AMAB author, or "assigned male at birth," beyond the racial and "stay in your lane" matters, is to be cognizant of the identifiers of sexuality or asexuality and the percentage of LGBTQ+ in the United States (4%). Some include: ACE for asexual; Cisgender, a person whose biological sex matches with their gender identity; and Polyamorous: A person who finds themselves romantically, physically, and/or sexually attracted to multiple individuals, and finds that pursuing multiple relationships is the most satisfying course of action in their lives.

Revolutionary Zeal Required

There is literally no field of study that is not being probed or scrubbed for racist, discriminatory tendencies and, hence, censure and erasure. Consider classical music, for example. According to Nebal Maysaud:

"It is time to let classical music die. Western classical music is not about culture. It's about whiteness. It's a combination of European traditions which serve the specious belief that whiteness has a culture—one that is superior to all others. Its main purpose is to be a cultural anchor for the myth of white supremacy."

Beethoven was actually a revolutionary in his time and place. Well, no more 4th Piano Concerto, I guess.

Math, architecture, Greek and Roman studies, physics, medicine are all undergoing scrutiny. In order to truly purge these and other fields from "Whiteness," a Red Guard mentality is likely needed going forward. Purging the United States of White Supremacy, White Saviorism, and Whiteness is a herculean task. That effort might be assisted by reading Making Civilizations: The World Before 600 (2020). Race, religion and violence have been powerful forces in the development of humanity. Completing the work of eradicating all three from society will take thousands of years and an evolutionary leap; or, perhaps, a world catastrophe.

CHAPTER 3: AMERICAN MINDS ARE ARTIFICIALLY INTELLIGENT

"I advocate the thesis which holds that the tendency towards totalitarianism is part of the essence of the machine, and originally proceeded from the realm of technology; that the tendency, inherent to every machine as such, to subjugate the world, to parasitically seize upon the fragments that have not yet been subjugated, to merge with other machines and to operate with them as pieces of a single, total machine: I maintain that this tendency represents the fundamental fact and that political totalitarianism, as horrible as it is, only represents an effect and variant of this fundamental technological fact. While the spokesmen of the technologically advanced world powers have been claiming for decades that they are engaged in resistance against the principle of totalitarianism (in the interest of the "free world"), their claims are fraudulent or, in the best cases, are the effect of a lack of intelligence, for the principle of totalitarianism is a technical principle and, as such, is not fought —nor will it ever be fought—by the "anti-totalitarians" From the times of the dictatorship we know that, from the moment when one considers that it is possible that one is under surveillance, one feels and behaves differently than one did before, that is, in a more conformist way, when not in an absolutely conformist way. The unverifiable possibility of being under surveillance has a decisive capacity for molding: it molds the entire population."

– Gunther Anders, The Obsolescence of Man, Volume II.

"The acceleration of innovation, made possible by an exponential increase in calculating power, led straight to a hyper-technological Ancien Regime where the positions to be occupied in the hierarchy of jobs, incomes, assets, education, living spaces, etc., depend on birth exactly as they did before the French Revolution. Thus, from the transhumanism of Silicon Valley there emerges not a post-human self but a very familiar figure, the aristocrat, having become cyber and with a head, cut off in 1789, that has grown back. Confidence in technology as a means of creating more liberty, more democracy, and less enslavement is belied once more by the truly deplorable actual results of this reproduction of power relations."

– Maurizio Lazzarato, Capital Hates Everyone

Artificial Intelligence: Adults

It is tempting to think that free-will exists. Unfortunately, it does not, particularly in America (tip of the hat to Baruch Spinoza writing in his Ethics). Taste in music (rap, rock, pop, etc.), fashion and food; political orientation whether left, right or center; what sports team to support, or vehicle to drive, or television series to watch is all supplied by media/corporations to American brains that are as malleable as silly putty. The mind easily succumbs to the totalitarian machinations of the American domestic/global capitalist network as its marketers, advertisers, and politicians/ideologues pound content into the brain via television news, hand-held computers/telephones, the world wide web, social media, and legacy media. Alberto J. L. Carrillo Canan believes that "the dominant technological forms determine the way we conceive reality, human life and mind."

How does one account for a meaningful life in American society? What would be contained in a meaningful life's ledger? How do you determine if you are free and not programmed? Two days of administered freedom at the end of the workweek? A new car? A two-week vacation at the beach? A mammoth flat screen television? A new iPhone? A new season of a television series on Netflix? A college degree? A mortgage on the house? A yearly bonus for productivity? The ability to vote for only two candidates for the

President of the United States? An opinion you really believe is yours?

All these "things" are supplied to you and all courtesy of the bio-capitalist, totalitarian machine. No one can escape it. Young or old, the American mind is captive to the totalitarian technological order. Ideas, products, news, and opinions are supplied, recycled/re-hashed and delivered. But what about the spontaneous protests and demands of, say, Black Lives Matter (BLM), you ask? Notice how quickly BLM's agenda was absorbed by the entire totalitarian capi-talist enterprise who made easy money available via donations to BLM activists, advertised their cause, and promised to hire more Blacks. BLM is now a fading blip on the American capitalist radar shot down by the capitalist totalitarian system. Indeed, BLM has cashed in. The same story/process is repeated over and over again no matter the issue or the protest or the time.

Not Your Opinion, Your Meaningless Life

"It does not matter whether someone who is expressing himself thinks that his expression is his own bona fide expression, or even if he asks himself 'is this my opinion or not?', or even if he does not even understand the question; in any case, what is not permit-ted is that what he expresses should be his own opinion; it must always be a supplied opinion. Even when it seems to be advisable to allow variations, they must be predictable variations on the pre-established theme…Most of those who lead meaningless lives are not even conscious of their misfortune. By way of the life that is imposed upon them they are prevented from perceiving its lack of meaning. That is why they cannot do anything to counteract this lack of meaning, either. Or, more precisely: even what they do to counteract it is something that is done to them, that is, something that is supplied to them," claims Anders.

According to Lazaratto, Google, Amazon, Facebook, Apple and Microsoft (plus consolidated media) are the masters guiding the behaviors of the governed. "By constantly soliciting one's attention—giving rise to an activity as absurd as compulsively consulting one's smartphone…they tirelessly fabricate and information designed to affect subjectivities circulating through billions of telephones, televisions, computers, tablets, whose connections envelop the planet in a thicker and thicker net."

It is not just the corporations though. Republicans, Democrats, the US Military, interest groups, and lobbyists (collectively, the neoliberal order) all get their products/messages on the airwaves and into the minds of the American human herd. The "masters" would likely be happier automating/digitizing American citizens/slaves.

Glutaraldehyde Fixation: Duh, What?

The digital dissection of the human being, individually and collectively, is proceeding apace. Uploading "the human" is no longer the stuff of science fiction. In a few generations, a parent may say to a child, "Hey, let's upload great grandpa and see/hear what he has to say." Why not pull the brain out of a dead body, preserve it in a special solution, and then mine it for memories that can be turned into 0's and 1's.

Macabre, you likely say, but the research is underway and funded. Ah, the beauty of capitalism! Consider the enterprising company Nectome. They are in the business of preserving the brains of the dead in hopes of digitally retrieving long term memories.

According to MIT Technology Review, "Nectome has received substantial support for its technology, however. It has raised $1 million in funding so far, including the $120,000 that Y Combinator provides to all the companies it accepts. It has also won a $960,000 federal grant from the US National Institute of Mental

Health for "whole-brain nanoscale preservation and imaging," the text of which foresees a "commercial opportunity in offering brain preservation" for purposes including drug research."

Tracking digital footprints and then converting them into behavioral models able to predict the next set of keystrokes, online and offline habits/geolocations, and spending preferences are well known practices undertaken by companies like Alphabet-Google. For example, today's software programs learn what words an individual uses to compose letters, articles, emails and once enough verbiage has been collated by the machine, a human writer can cut out the thought process used to seek out an adjective, a noun or verb. Just one more human function taken away from the brain and absorbed by the software in the machine.

In some not to distant future, the human mind/person will be digitized and exist in a bio-machine.

Artificial Intelligence: Youngsters

What kind of adults are being created by the totalitarian technological education system? I used to believe that an innovative education based on critical thinking and systems analysis, beginning from about 4th grade level through high school, might provide a check on the monstrous technology/system that is dominating every facet of life.

But having experience education as a teacher in both public and private settings, I have stopped believing that youngsters are going to be anything more than unconscious routers, servers, or surveillance sensors for the totalitarian machine. They will be more conformist than their parents or the adults that are nominally in charge of the United States.

The teachers/system set a pace that is relentless which means there is no time for a pause or a gaze into thoughtfulness/thinking. It is not learning but programming that the students are subjected to.

I asked an 8th grader recently what he would change about school if he could. "I would not teach boring," he responded. "All the students I know don't like school because it is so boring. Teachers need to change. We are not learning anything," he said in frustration. Add to this the crazy reality that the World Wide Web is barely used by teachers for science, math, politics, history, or geography. It is largely a cut and paste enterprise with teachers selecting documents from the Web, printing them out in paper form, and distributing them to their classes.

The public and private schools I have been in (K-12) are a dizzying mishmash of things and frenetic human activity: wires, electronic white boards; non-ergonomic 19th Century desks and chairs (plastic and aluminum); Apple iPads; robotic parts; Lego's; classrooms adorned with cardboard signs with annoying cliches (You Are Special or The Future Starts Here); laptops; boxes of crayons and pencils; decade old paper files in equally old file cabinets; hallway banners proclaiming "Award Winning School, 2020"; half empty classrooms due to the COVID19 Pandemic; virtual students on Microsoft Teams at home who log in and leave the class, never responding to a teacher's question; layers of management (assistant principals); constant teacher meetings/professional development courses; waves of substitute teachers; and curriculum focused solely on achieving high scores on a State's Standards of Learning.

Many of the software programs used for learning, particularly in grades K-8, are equivalent to an arcade game or pinball machine: carnival music accompanies the student through, say, a science lesson. Answer correctly and the sound of a bell or whistle can be heard. Answer a question wrong and later a "power up" function gives you a chance to correct your mistake and add points. There are also competitive learning games that students participate in. Cartoonish software programs like Kahoot, Nearpod, Gizmo, Quizizz, Brain Pop all amp up the level of excitement to create an experience similar to a popular video game.

I was substituting in an 8th grade science class recently where the subject being taught was weather. I asked the students if the teacher was using the National Oceanic and Atmospheric Administration (NOAA.GOV) website to help them learn about the subject. They looked at me like I was an alien creature. "What's that," one student responded. I explained but to no avail as I had to get to the instructions left by the teacher that I was to follow.

Red Guards

I was substitute teaching in a classroom full of 8th graders (12-13 years old, I am 65) not long ago. I was talking about something or other and inadvertently pulled my mask down below my lips for a few moments exposing my face. It was an error in judgement, a mistake for which I had no excuse (I am fully vaccinated for COVID19 and was 6 feet away from the nearest student). When I was finished speaking to the class, I pulled my mask back up and thought nothing of it.

Turns out that I was surreptitiously being recorded by a student who turned the video over to an assistant principal. I was nearly released for the mistake but the assistant principal that first received the video argued on my behalf to the principal and I was kept on staff. My punishment was to write a memo for record/file explaining what I had done. The next step was to apologize to the 8th graders in person.

I thought immediately of Mao's Red Guards:

"The first Red Guards groups were made up of students, ranging from as young as elementary school children up to university students…The Red Guards also publicly humiliated teachers, monks, former landowners or anyone else suspected of being "counter-revolutionary.""

What happened to, "Hey, Mr. Stanton, you need to put your mask back up."

Not long ago, I was in a class with a new substitute teacher, fresh out of college. He politely asked the class of 6th graders what time the class ended. What he got was this from a student, "You are the substitute, you should know."

CHAPTER 4: BIDEN'S SHAMEFUL PUSH FOR WAR WITH CHINA AND RUSSIA: IGNORING HISTORY, DENYING REALITY

"One of the most delightful things about Americans is that they have absolutely no historical memory."

– Zhou Enlai

'In the autumn of 1862, the governments of France and Great Britain proposed to Russia, in a formal but not in an official way, the joint recognition by European powers of the independence of the Confederate States of America. My immediate answer was: 'I will not cooperate in such action; and I will not acquiesce. On the contrary, I shall accept the recognition of the independence of the Confederate States by France and Great Britain as a casus belli for Russia. And in order that the governments of France and Great Britain may understand that this is no idle threat; I will send a Pacific fleet to San Francisco and an Atlantic fleet to New York. Sealed orders to both Admirals were given. My fleets arrived at the American ports, there was no recognition of the Confederate States by Great Britain and France. The American rebellion was put down, and the great American Republic continues. All this I did because of love for my own dear Russia, rather than for love of the American Republic. I acted thus because I understood that Russia would have a more serious task to perform if the American Republic, with advanced industrial development were broken up and Great Britain should be left in control of most branches of modern industrial development.''

– Czar Alexander II

Americans are exact replicas of Stoner Jeff Spicoli, a character played by Sean Penn in the movie Fast Times at Ridgemont High.

The new "hot" war novel 2034 co-authored by Admiral James Stavridis (USN, Ret.) and Elliot Ackerman (US combat veteran) depicts a future war between the US and China. 2034 the movie cannot be far behind or perhaps the rights to convert the novel into film has already been transacted between the two august military veterans and Hollywood agents. My bet is that this will be cameo filled movie with all the big-name stars of the day, sort of like The Longest Day, a movie depicting the D-Day invasion during WWII.

A similar themed World War III novel was written by Sir John Hackett in 1985 during the height of first Cold War pitting the United States against the former Soviet Union. There are scores of novels on the subject, many of which can be found here at Goodreads. What is the point of these tomes? What are the Las Vegas gambling odds on WWIII taking place? There are, indeed, gambling sites like Sportsbettingdime.com and @Everythingodds that will at least entertain the probability of WWIII and when it might happen.

Moral Derangement

What a coincidence that 2034 has been released just as President Joe Biden and other US government officials are is ramping up the political and economic pressure on China and Russia through sanctions and incendiary verbiage. Pentagon war planners likely consult these works to see if there is any useful information that can be included in the "real" WWIII plans. Who is the target audience for these doomsday works? The World Socialist Website, in a scathing review, makes a case that the preferred readership is policymakers in Washington, DC, defense contractors, think tanks and the US military writ large. They also point out that there are no works of art–books or films—recently produced that hardily critique any presidential administration about the folly of nuclear war with China or Russia. Everyone loses in that scenario.

"A normal person, that is, one for whom moral derangement is not a professional requirement, would read Stavridis' book with horror and do everything to avoid the massive level of death it depicts. But the fact is that, for its intended audience within the Beltway and the Pentagon, the tactical nuclear exchanges depicted in the book, constitute, in the words of Dr. Strangelove's Gen. Buck Turgidson, "Getting our hair mussed"—an entirely acceptable consequence of the use of nuclear weapons. Stanley Kubrick's masterful Dr. Strangelove, Sidney Lumet's Fail Safe, and, more obliquely, John Frankenheimer's Seven Days in May (all released in 1964) were scathing critiques of the military and of nuclear war. No such critical works are being written and produced today, and ground has been ceded to Stavridis' sanitized depiction of nuclear war from the standpoint of a practitioner."

Fungus

One of the best techniques to prepare for war is to turn an enemy into some sort of sinister fungus and through the use of government propaganda planted in the mainstream media, prepare the dismally educated public for war. Or gin up stories of Russia and China's meddling in US elections (enough already!). US propaganda must avoid any reference to past friendly or helpful interest-based relations, or conflicts, between the three nations. In this case, Americans are not to be informed that China, Russia, and the United States have very similar economic and human interests. What good would a nuclear—or conventional war–do any of the three powers?

What do US policymakers and military leaders fear? The United States has a string of global military bases and intelligence outposts to which China and Russia have no real answer for, save for maybe nuclear weapons and espionage-cyber-information operations (the US has 17 well funded intelligence agencies to work the latter problem). Plus, the world knows that the US National Security Agency has unmatched signals intelligence (SIGINT) capability to eavesdrop on just about any international communications. Moreover, the US has air, space, sea (an undersea) assets that neither China nor Russia can match without the use of suicidal tactical nuclear weapons. Land forces are a different story: Iraq, Afghanistan, Somalia; and, going way back, Vietnam have shown that it is capable to bog down US Army forces in irregular warfare. The US spends nearly $1.2 trillion per year on all its military, intelligence, and homeland security needs. At this moment it is modernizing all its strategic nuclear forces and adding intermediate range nuke missiles to the mix. All of this is ostensibly aimed at "Great Powers" Russia and China. It's as if the Pentagon brass wants to fight "real" opponents with air-combat, amphibious landings and tanks battles.

Any avid readers in the US taking a look at the New York Times or Washington Post (two mouthpieces for the US government) might think that the US is already at war, at least economically and via espionage, with China and Russia. But it would probably come as a surprise to most Americans that, in the midst of a new Cold War, Russia ranked third in oil exports to the US in 2020.

According to Bloomberg News:

"Even as Washington champions energy independence and warns European allies against becoming too dependent on Moscow, American refineries are buying more of the country's oil than ever before…Deprived of access to Venezuelan crude by US sanctions on the regime of Nicolás Maduro, and facing reduced shipments from OPEC nations since the cartel cut output, US refiners turned to Russian oil in 2020 to fill the gap. The buying spree, combined with sharply lower Saudi shipments, catapulted Russia into the position of third-largest oil supplier to the US last year."

Russia was also vital to the Union cause during the US civil war. There is a tendency to think that the US civil war was fought in isolation without any concern of the powers of the day in Europe or Russia(1860-1865). In the geopolitical drama of those years, Britain and France were maneuvering to take advantage of the worst-case scenario of the American Civil War: a victory by the slave-based economy of the Confederacy. They intended to recognize the Confederacy as a distinct country. The perception that Czar Alexander II might come to the aid of the Abraham Lincoln and the Union was disconcerting to Great Britain and France. While the Russian fleet docked in the San Francisco and New York harbors at the time might not have been formidable foes to the surface fleets of Great Britain and France, that and other maneuvers by US diplomat Cassius Clay(appointed by Abraham Lincoln as ambassador to Russia) significantly aided the cause of the Union forces.

Vinegar and Global Corporations in China

China is home to a museum that pays tribute to WWII General "Vinegar" Joe Stilwell. Fluent in Chinese he was loosely in charge of all allied forces in the Burma-China-India theater of operations during WWII. Those allies included British and Chinese soldiers. Mao Tse Tung and Zhou Enlai would ultimately put their Red Army under his command. According to Smithsonian Magazine,

"…The Stilwell Museum in Chongqing, China, where the general lived while liaising with Chiang Kai-Shek, then fighting both the Japanese and a Communist insurgency that would spiral into China's long and brutal Civil War, ending in the establishment of the Peoples Republic. While Stilwell was there he grew increasingly disenchanted with corruption and subterfuge in Chiang's Nationalist government, ultimately opening communication with the Red Army under Mao Zedong, earning him hero status in contemporary China."

What do these global corporations have in common? Boeing, Walmart, Apple, McDonalds, National Basketball Association, Ford, and Koch Industries are just seven members of the US-China Business Council which lists scores of other American organizations to include law firms, pharmaceutical companies, financial houses, and consultancies that operate in China. Fly on a commercial aircraft lately? Components of the airplane are likely made in China. Likewise, there is the US-Russia Business Council with big names sponsoring the group like Caterpillar, Citi, Microsoft, Chevron, Exxon-Mobil, and General Electric.

Does the US want to nuke its own corporations?

Finally, US soldiers met Chinese ground troops in 1950 during the bloody and oft forgotten Korean War. That conflict has still not been settled by peace treaty and resulted in a stalemate. Thinking about waging a successful conventional land war with China is the province of lunatics.

Historical Lesson from 1918-1919

But let's return to the US Army's experience fighting the forces of a Leon Trotsky-led Red Army in 1918-1919. That return reminds of Vietnam, Iraq and Afghanistan. US soldiers fought with bravery but they were given no specific guidance from Woodrow Wilson in Washington, DC. The US warfighters were caught in a quagmire: the Russian Civil War was afoot and the end of WWI changed the political landscape of Europe and Russia. Troops had no idea what they were doing in Russia. According to Smithsonian Magazine:

"'Events moved so fast in 1918, they made the mission moot,' says James Nelson, author of The Polar Bear Expedition. They kept these guys in isolated, naked positions well into 1919. The biggest complaint you heard from the soldiers was, 'No one can tell us why we're here,' especially after the Armistice. Historians tend to see Wilson's decision to send troops to Russia as one of his worst wartime decisions, and a foreshadowing of other poorly planned American interventions in foreign countries in the century since…'It didn't really achieve anything—it was ill-conceived,' says Nelson. The lessons were there that could've been applied in Vietnam and could've been applied in Iraq. Jonathan Casey, director of archives at the World War I Museum, agrees. 'We didn't have clear goals in mind politically or militarily,' he says. 'We think we have an interest to protect, but it's not really our interest to protect, or at least to make a huge effort at it. Maybe there are lessons we should've learned.'"

CHAPTER 5: THE HELL OF THE SAME: CAPITALISM BREAKS DOWN AND HOMOGENIZES LIFE, DISCONNECTS THE PAST, PRESENT AND FUTURE

"Capitalism is often interpreted as a religion. However, if religion is understood in terms of Religare, as something that binds, then capitalism is anything but a religion because it lacks any force to assemble, to create community…And what is essential to religion is contemplative rest, but this is the antithesis of Capital. Capital never rests. It is in its nature that it must always work and continue moving. To the extent that they lose the capacity for contemplative rest, humans conform to Capital. The distinction between the sacred and profane is also an essential characteristic of religion. The sacred unites those things and values that give validity to a community. The formation of community is its essential trait. Capitalism, by contrast, erases the distinction between the sacred and the profane by totalizing the profane. It makes everything comparable to everything else and thus equal to everything else. Capitalism brings forth a hell of the same."

– Byung-Chul Han, The Disappearance of Rituals.

"Western tradition both underscores and denigrates matter—a duality more than evident in the history of subjugated persons: those un-consenting women, children, slaves, and aboriginal peoples who have been used as mere property and all others who have been merely used by others, rather than beheld as thinking, desiring agents. In our greed for power and novelty, is there anything that might escape the inevitable obsolescence of use? Once our labor, our health, our traditions and knowledge, our emotions, our very thoughts become commodities, they are stripped of life and growth…The environmental catastrophe we think of as the ruin of nature is in fact the ruin of human nature, the end of our sustainable life on Earth"

– Susan Stewart, The Ruins Lesson: Meaning and Material in Western Culture.

In the English lexicon of the day, it is verboten to mention that some inspiration, sense of wonder, or a pause to reflect on a passage from the texts of ancient myth and/or religion is a positive. You run the risk at a Washington, DC, cocktail party of being ostracized if you praise Pope Francis for washing people's feet or visiting Iraq, discussing the myths of the Saints, or even the tales of more ancient deities of Rome, Athens, Babylon, and pharaonic Egypt. Who cannot but like the Greek story of Orpheus and Eurydice?

Instead, its "Hey! See the latest American Idol? How about that language in the federal budget that I got in there for my client? Why do you care about these f*&^%$# children's tales and that Pope guy? What's that good for?"

Vicars of Capitalism

The gimpy Pope, with one kidney, visited the Iraqi cities of Ur, Baghdad, Mosul, and Najaf, among others. Even Hezbollah lauded the Pope's calls for unity and peace in Iraq, a country essentially destroyed by the number one capitalist country on the planet, the United States. His faith and mission to unify people carried him to a demolished and barely functional Iraq. If that cannot be considered inspirational, that means that capitalism has successfully commodified the Pope turning him and his likeness into a key chain or a pen. Which one of the following vicars of 21st Century capitalism would undertake such a Pope-like endeavor: Jeff Bezos (Amazon), Bill Gates (Microsoft, retired), Elon Musk (Tesla, Space X), Richard Branson (Virgin Atlantic). Security issues, you say. Well, what enterprising remnant of the Islamic State would not have liked to take a shot at the Pope?

Exploitation of the Many by the Many: It is Your Job!

Sure, the ancient myths, religious beliefs—to include Islam, Christianity, Judaism, Hindi, Buddhism—can be positioned as quaint fairy tales with silly rituals, and not worthy of the brain power expended in reading them. But who can't but be inspired by the Babylonian Epic of Gilgamesh, the Egyptian Tale of Sinhue and The Four Vedas (Ka by Roberto Calasso is a brilliant text on the Vedas). Texts like these tell the stories of early humanity and are rich in color, allegory, and of course myth. They go beyond the major religions of the book as explorations that might as well be on the moon for their time.

It is not possible to read these texts straight through like a sprinter running the 100 meters. Many pauses are required to think through what has just been read. It is akin to a long contemplative walk where frequent stops are made to look around, to ponder, to be amazed. It hits you when you realize the ancients, the authors-editors-translators of the texts are all part of an interconnected world in which humans seek meaning.

Capitalism has little time for sub-surface thought, for depth. It is all about how fast one can consume, as Han indicates in his book. One is trained in the capitalist system and subsequently pushed into the ruthless routine of consumption and competition with all humans beings encountered through life's assembly line.

Capitalism is the practice of exploitation of the self and others. The focus on Wall Street, Bezos/Musk or capitalism and its past history is ill placed. No, the worst and most damaging part of the cult of capitalism is that it quietly plants a seed of destructive exploitation in each and every person's head that says, "It's ok to exploit everyone, everywhere at all times. I will sell my soul. Everyone does it. I'll get mine." There is always money to made on any concept, emotion, historical wrong, death, etc. Family, friends, coworkers, teachers, children, professors are easy targets for exploitation. Watch television, surf the web, check your hand-held, go to the movies, read the newspapers (online), play with Tik Tok. The gears of capitalism will grind on and will never stop until someone, or something, presses the stop button (even the Pandemic could not stop capitalism).

Above all capitalism is manically authoritarian and indoctrinating. It slowly crushes any ideas, beliefs not conducive to turning people into information speed freaks who do not realize they possess only administrative freedom. Capitalism molds everyone and everything into malleable forms with minor variations which appeal to the majority of society, consisting of the unfree consumer, who has been pummeled with marketing slogans and television commercials, and advertising pop ups/click bait on the computer.

Capitalism also seeks to stifle freedom of speech unless it is digital speech maintained in bits and bytes and approved for entertainment value. Capitalism has turned people into fireflies in the dark night: A brief flash of chemical light and the creature is gone. A person's ability to think disappears as quickly as the fireflies' light and, perhaps, so does its existence.

I currently feel for the Social Justice vanguard. Capitalism will crush that movement too. For the moment, the issue is hot and trendy. In fact, capitalism applauds the erasure of Western Civilization's history. Guilt sells. There is always a tidy profit to be made using destroying the past to create a future with a new or no identity or history, and no vocabulary.

There is Nothing Below the Surface

How the World Ends

One cannot engage in an in-depth conversation about these issues
unless you fork over $100,000 to a college or university to discuss
them. But wait! Ancient texts? Religion? Literature? These are
studies that are probably in the Liberal Arts/Humanities depart-
ments which are being strangled of funds. But that is all part of the
capitalist plan. As Henry Giroux points out

> "Education within the last three decades has diminished
> rapidly in its capacities to educate young people to be re-
> flective, critical, and socially engaged agents. Despite all
> attempts to degrade the value and purpose of education,
> the notion of education as the primary register of the larger
> culture persists. Yet, under a neoliberal regime, the utopian
> possibilities formerly associated with public and higher
> education as a public good capable of promoting social
> equality and supporting democracy have become too dan-
> gerous for the apostles of neoliberalism. Critical thought
> and the imaginings of a better world present a direct threat
> to a neoliberal paradigm in which the future must always
> replicate the present in an endless circle in which capital
> and the identities that legitimate it merge with each other
> into what might be called a dead zone."

No Closure

Combine the push of the Critical Theorists with capitalism's doc-
trines and you have got a quicker, more "legitimate" way to purge
Liberal Arts/Humanities or White history. Critical Theorists have
played right into capitalism's hands. "Just another means to erase
the past," the capitalists will say. "Just another way to unmoor a
large swath of the populations. There's money to be made in Guilt.
You know, we will sell it like we did diet cola or sugar free gum.
Wipe your guilt away with brand X." The capitalist process involved is sad. No one can see it, or acknowledge it.

How the World Ends

Capitalism has the patience of Job and ensures that nothing is really complete, according to Han. One is always pushing to an incomplete future from a foggy present and unknown past:

"We are losing the capacity for closure and this means that life is becoming purely an additive process. For something to die life must find its own closure. If life is deprived of any possibility of closure it will end in non-time. Because it rushes from sensation to the next, even perception is now incapable of closure…Where everything is connected, no closure is possible. The loss of forms of completions that accompanies overproduction and overconsumption lead to systemic collapse. The neoliberal imperative of optimization and performance does not allow for any completion. Everything is provisional and incomplete; nothing is final and conclusive…The We that is capable of joint action is also a form of closure. Today, it disintegrates into egos who voluntarily exploit themselves as entrepreneurs of their own selves…Flexibility is enforced by the ruthless destruction of bonds."

Capitalism is not a definable thing. I was walking outside here in Northern Virginia and heard the humming, electric buzz of a million Cicadas. It was not possible to see all the critters parked in the trees. But they were there, yelling/buzzing in their own way. I thought then of a dense fog in which nothing can really be seen. Only the noise, a cacophony of strange creatures can be heard.

And then I thought that capitalism is really some sort of creature, present since humanity started to value things, people, animals, clothes, voices, trade. It is ancient. It is not a system imposed by some alien force. Capitalism is the Sirens from Greek mythology

Maybe it is a return to symbols, rituals and ancient tales that can help us escape the fog of life that capitalism produces. If we can't find meaning from ancients that searched for it when the world was largely unknown to them, and applaud their effort, then where else might we find it. In the stars, solar systems long dead from the past. Or how about self-help books or the next war coming up to provide meaning.

I don't have a good answer.

CHAPTER 6: WHAT IS THE UNITED STATES OF AMERICA? A MILITARY DEMOCRACY

"Military leader, council, assembly of the people are the organs of gentile society developed into military democracy: military, since war and organization for war have now become regular functions of national life. Their neighbors' wealth excites the greed of peoples who already see in the acquisition of wealth one of the main aims of life. They are barbarians: they think it more easy and in fact more honorable to get riches by pillage than by work. War, formerly waged only in revenge for injuries or to extend territory that had grown too small, is now waged simply for plunder and becomes a regular industry. Not without reason the bristling battlements stand menacingly about the new fortified towns; in the moat at their foot yawns the grave of the gentile constitution, and already they rear their towers into civilization and similarly in the interior. The wars of plunder increase the power of the supreme military leader and the subordinate commanders..."

Frederick Engels, Origins of the Family, Private Property, and the State

"The label full spectrum dominance implies that US forces are able to conduct prompt, sustained,and synchronized operations with combinations of forces tailored to specific situations and with access to and freedom to operate in all domains—land, sea, air, space, and information. Additionally, given the global nature of our interests and obligations, the United States must maintain its overseas presence forces and the ability to rapidly project power worldwide in order to achieve full spectrum dominance. Achieving full spectrum dominance means the joint force will fulfill its primary purpose— victory in war—as well as achieving success across the full range of operations, but it does not mean that we will win without cost or difficulty." Joint Vision 2020, 2000

"The United States must retain overmatch—the combination of capabilities in sufficient scale to prevent enemy success and to ensure that America's sons and daughters will never be in a fair fight. Overmatch strengthens our diplomacy and permits us to shape the international environment to protect our interests. To retain military overmatch the United States must restore our ability to produce innovative capabilities, restore the readiness of our forces for major war, and grow the size of the force so that it is capable of operating at sufficient scale and for example duration to win across a range of scenarios."

National Security Strategy of the United States, 2017

So the United States wants to play hardball with China; and, naturally Russia, by resurfacing the Cold War era doctrine of Containment, along with Nuclear Triad upgrades, a 500 ship US Navy, new Long Range Bombers—and a replacement for the F-35— hypersonic weapons and, of course, more bodies for the all-volunteer US military. That means more dollars have to be funneled to the Pentagon and its suppliers. But there is more: US military initiatives in Artificial Intelligence, Quantum Computing, Autonomous Combat Drones (undersea and air), Space Based Weapons, and Synthetic Biology all add to the truckloads of dollars needed to take on China and Russia, never mind North Korea and Iran.

The fiscal year 2021 defense budget comes in at a whopping $740.5 billion dollars. But there is more security to be had: The Department of Homeland Security will spend roughly $50 billion and the Department of Justice (houses the FBI) $30 billion. US intelligence agencies are expected to spend approximately $85 billion in 2021 with a new focus on China. That adds up to about $905 billion dollars.

But let's stop our immediately scheduled militarist programming to talk a bit about the failure to act on intelligence reports and the storming of America's secular temple, the iconic US Capitol building which houses America's elected representatives. You can be forgiven if 911 comes to mind.

WTF!

Am I getting this right? $905 billion to fight the bad men and women of Russia, China, Iran and North Korea—and let's not forget the foreign terrorists—but the paramilitary forces and military forces of the United States could not stop a largely angry white mob from overtaking the US Capitol while the House and Senate were in joint session confirming the electoral count in favor of the 46th President of the United States Joe Biden, who defeated Donald Trump in the 2020 election.

Are you kidding me?

The movie is in the works, no doubt. Who will star? Maybe it will be akin to the Alamo only this time the reinforcements arrive on time and save the day. You have the heroic capitol police dude who led protesters away form the Senate chambers. There will be the tragic relationship in which a bullet connects a capitol law enforcement official to a woman trying to climb through a broken window into a hallway whose offices members of congress were hiding. She dies, he's under investigation. Well, apparently no one tried to get through that window afterwards.

The tragic deaths of two capitol police officers will be acted out: a couple of scenes will be shown from a fight with protestors in which one officer was hit in the head with a fire extinguisher and who collapsed upon return to HQ and died; the other from suicide, performed in the aftermath of the security debacle.

Merchants of Death, For Real

The USA also maintains its status as the number one arms dealer in the world with distasteful customers including Saudi Arabia and Egypt. According to Forbes, "US bombs, aircraft, attack helicopters, and other military equipment have been used in [Yemen for] indiscriminate attacks that have killed thousands of civilians, enabled destruction of civilian infrastructure, and bolstered a blockade that has impeded the provision of vital humanitarian supplies. The result has been up to 100,000 unnecessary deaths and the placement of millions of Yemenis on the brink of famine. In Egypt, torture, unlawful confinement, and forced disappearances are now routine, under what many analysts view as the most repressive regime in the history of that nation. In addition, the Egyptian regime has engaged in forced displacement, strikes on civilians, and other abuses in its anti-terror campaign in the northern Sinai, all the while attempting to hide these abuses from the media and foreign governments, including major aid suppliers like the United States."

And there is no end in sight to what has become the premier Military Democracy in world history.

According to the Project on Government Oversight:

> "Defense spending increased sharply in the Trump years and is now substantially higher than it was during the Korean or Vietnam War eras or during the massive military buildup President Ronald Reagan oversaw in the 1980s. Today, it consumes well over half of the nation's discretionary budget, which just happens to also pay for a wide array of urgently needed priorities ranging from housing, job training, and alternative energy programs to public health and infrastructure building. At a time when pandemics, high unemployment, racial inequality, and climate change pose the greatest threats to our safety and security, this allocation of resources should be considered unsus-

tainable. Unfortunately, the Pentagon and the arms industry have yet to get that memo. Defense company executives recently assured a Washington Post reporter that they are "unconcerned" about or consider unlikely the possibility that a Biden administration would significantly reduce Pentagon spending."

Add it all up and you are looking at billions in cash that has to be printed, or found, every year to sustain and enhance the massive US national security/defense machine even as the United States is getting hammered by the COVID-19 Pandemic which is, in turn, crippling its economy.

If that weren't enough to be concerned about, there is the dicey constitutional matter of the former sitting president (Donald Trump) who contacted the governor of the US State of Georgia and the speaker of the state house in Pennsylvania in an unprecedented attempt at an "art of the deal" coup to overturn the results of the 2020 presidential election that saw the defeat of Trump by Democrat Joe Biden. A defeat that Trump and many Republicans refused to acknowledge going so far as to file baseless lawsuits seeking to overturn the election. What Trump and his supporters are doing to degrade representative democracy is as close to treason as is possible.

At any rate, what's the point of the United States spending billions of dollars—some estimates as high as 1.2 trillion—on national security/defense when its healthcare system, critical infrastructure (bridges, sewage pipes, roads, etc.), small to mid-sized businesses, and social safety nets—even the constitutional order— are collapsing?

Maybe it is all part of the plan. President Joe Biden has shown that he is part of that plan too,

How China Became an Evil Doer: Rabid Imperialist Running Dog, Peter Navarro

Why is China being led to the electric chair? Well, there's America's number one anti-Chinese imperialist running dog to thank for that, Peter Navarro, White House trade and manufacturing advisor to President Donald Trump. Navarro is a rabid, foam-at-the-mouth Chinese hate machine, a racist by any other name. His book Death By China borders on lunacy. According to Vox:

> "Navarro doesn't only want to crackdown on China's economic practices in order to boost the American economy. He also believes slowing China's growth is essential to taming its military might and ambitions for global dominance.On this front, his views — which include calling for the US to colonize the moon with American-style capitalism before China turns it into a communist stronghold — become particularly difficult to follow. [He warns] the reader against ever purchasing Chinese products [and claims that] unscrupulous Chinese entrepreneurs are flooding world markets with a range of bone-crushing, cancer-causing, flammable, poisonous, and otherwise lethal products, foods, and drugs. At one point, Navarro asks the reader to engage in a cautionary thought experiment and — using a military phrase popularized during the Vietnam War — imagine that your best friend is fragged when the [Chinese-made] cell phone in his chest pocket explodes and sends bone shrapnel into his heart.'"

Navarro was a key figure in the development of Trump's 2017 National Security Strategy (NSS) which laid the groundwork for the Pentagon's National Defense Strategy (NDS) and yet another doctrine with an acronym: Great Power Competition or GPC. Particular emphasis was placed on China: The alleged threatening commercial investments in Central and South America, claims on the South China Sea and remote islands, and the $178 to $225 billion they spent on their military in 2019. And Russia has been naughty too: It secured its strategic interests by taking back Crimea (prime Navy base there which the US was eyeing for itself), intervening to protect its interests in Georgia, and supporting rebels in Ukraine and the hapless regime in Syria (where Russia has interests in the form of military bases).

"It is just business," as Michael Corleone said in the movie Godfather II. It was just that when the US invaded Iraq in 2003 (a failure by all accounts). But it's just fine when the US makes moves on the geopolitical chessboard, not other nations. The attitude goes something like this: "How dare they try to mess with the post-WWII order created by the USA."

GPC, No More GWOT

The NDS normally follows the president's NSS as the Pentagon has to outline how it will meet the Commander in Chief's vision. The NDS was also pushed out by the Pentagon in 2017 with then Secretary of Defense Jim Mattis being the lead cheerleader. He claimed that the era of the Global War on Terror (GWOT) was something that belonged in the dustbin of history. According to Defense One, "The National Defense Strategy declares a decisive shift in America's security priorities, away from the age of ISIS-level terrorism and toward a return to great-power competition with regional giants China and Russia. This shift, Pentagon planners say, will require a 'more lethal, resilient, and rapidly innovating' military that can regain the overwhelming advantage the United States once held over those rivals and lesser adversaries such as Iran and North Korea."

So the USA may stagger into a war with China thanks to a well placed anti-Chinese kook (Navarro) in the White House who was in on the development of both the NSS and NDS of 2017. The Pentagon and Defense Industrial base are for anything that'll get them more dollars. So China is the #1 totalitarian monster of the day.

And they say one person can't make a difference.

Maybe Boeing, Walmart and Apple—who invest heavily in Chinese supply chains and technical know-how—might have something to say about the GPC.

Anyway, let's say that the US military suddenly vanished. What would America be then? It would be a Paramilitary and Carceral Democracy.

The USA is a Military Democracy that refuses to adequately take care of its people. Is that really worth fighting for?

CHAPTER 7: THE UNITED STATES FACES IRREPARABLE DAMAGE IN A COLD OR HOT CONVENTIONAL WAR WITH CHINA AND ITS ALLIES

"Overall, the decline in US war-fighting advantages does not mean China can win a war that the United States is willing to fight. By 2025, a war could be a military standoff, with major weapon-platform losses on both sides, in addition to losses in cyberspace and space. Yet neither side would fare so much worse than the other that it would feel compelled to concede, raising the probability that a war would be both severe and long. Such a war could be decided by economic costs, domestic political effects, and international responses.Russia would be eager to help China make up for lost oil and gas supplies, though not for free. In addition, Russian arms could make up somewhat for Chinese military losses and expenditures (e.g., aircraft and air defense), though it would take time for them to be operationalized…

As for other Chinese "allies," North Korea is even more unpredictable than Russia.Although North Korea no longer has the conventional military capability to invade and defeat South Korea, it could use missiles against South Korea or Japan; although Seoul would almost certainly not enter a war against China in any case,Tokyo's options would be complicated by North Korean belligerence. A conflict between China and the United States could disturb the greater Middle East by providing an opening for heightened violence from Islamist-extremist and anti-Israel groups (ISIS, al Qaeda, Hamas, and Hezbollah). Middle East difficulties could place additional demands on US naval and air forces at a moment when more of them are needed in the Western Pacific."

RAND Corporation: War with China

"Our adversaries are not just going to let us go to the fight uncontested; we're going to have to fight our way across the ocean or under the ocean or in the air."

Former Commandant of the Marine Corps Gen. Robert Neller

It was clear that none of the grand brains in former administration of Donald Trump were thinking systematically about the costs of containing China; i.e., waging a Cold War against a nation of 1.4 billion people or actually fomenting a hot conventional war in the Western Pacific? Now that Joe Biden is the president of the United States and Tony Blinken his Secretary of State, they are following the tired tropes reminiscent of the language of that was employed during the USA vs USSR Cold War that saturated the consciousness of the American people and its Western European comrades.

Consider Biden's recent statement on China, " After Beijing imposed the new national security law in Hong Kong, Biden vowed in a statement to "Prohibit US companies from abetting repression and supporting the Chinese Communist Party's surveillance state" and to "impose swift economic sanctions" should freedom of speech of US citizens and entities be harmed. Also, Biden was one of the first prominent US politicians to congratulate Taiwan's President Tsai Ing-wen on her reelection and inauguration."

Here's an excerpt from Pompeo's recent speech on China:

"That the only way…the only way to truly change communist China is to act not on the basis of what Chinese leaders say, but how they behave. And you can see American policy responding to this conclusion. President Reagan said that he dealt with the Soviet Union on the basis of "trust but verify." When it comes to the CCP, I say we must distrust and verify… We know too, we know too that not all Chinese students and employees are just normal students and workers that are coming here to make a little bit of money and to garner themselves some knowledge. Too many of them come here to steal our intellectual property and to take this back to their country."

Biden, and his entire administration are channeling Pompeo.

Oh, you mean the Chinese version of the Israeli Art Students?

When the Berlin Wall came tumbling down and the fog of propaganda on both sides lifted, we all learned that the Soviet menace was not the evil or capable goliath it was made out to be. Though not a paper tiger given its nuclear arsenal, the Soviet Union's conventional forces were largely ill fed, under equipped and spread too thin. China is not the Soviet Union of the old Cold War years. It is a 21st Century force to be negotiated with and partnered with,not warred against by the United States. Its media outlets like Xinhuanet, China Daily and search engine Baidu (similar toRussia's RT and Sputnik and Yandex) have global readership/usage in the millions. The US does not dominate the open source news/propaganda through US/Western global outlets as it once did during the legacy Cold War.

China can play that new Cold War propaganda game now too. Consider China's annual report on human rights abuses in the United States. The validity of such a report can be questioned as propaganda, but it's out there on the World Wide Web for consumption and can't be deleted. Besides, it is not everyday you can watch videos of US police/paramilitary forces wounding its citizens as they protest for justice, or watch the murder of George Floyd, with knee on neck, begging not to be killed by a police officer. It is tough to counter those images when proclaiming "land of the free, home of the brave." I'm no apologist for China or Russia just as Boeing Corporation doesn't apologize for its business in China.

Make no mistake. The Chinese and Russians are masterful HUMINT (human intelligence) operatives and information warfare artists. They engage in cyberspace operations and media influence operations in the USA and abroad. They are,indeed, worthy competitors in these venues. But is this gamesmanship between nations a justifiable cause for a new cold or hot war? Besides, I'll take the National Security Agency's SIGINT (signals intelligence) capabilities and US information/psychological operations skills any day over what the Chinese and Russians have.Everyone tries to dig in the other's sandbox. Such is the province and practice of all capable nations like the USA, Russia,and China.

War with China: Pakistan's Role?

"Communist China entered the conflict at "frozen Chosin," shifting the war's momentum again. In a surprise attack, more than 100,000 Chinese troops trapped American forces in some of the harshest, most remote territory of the region—in temperatures that regularly fell to 25 degrees below zero. In a place where it was too frigid to dig foxholes without explosives and bulldozers, combatants piled frozen bodies in lieu of sandbags. Feet froze into blocks of ice inside boots. Even bullet wounds sometimes froze, keeping soldiers from bleeding out until they went inside heated tents," according to History.com.

A hot conventional war with China would require reinstatement of the draft in the United States.

The People's Liberation Army of the 1950s is far more capable in 2020 and is the largest in the world. Its military personnel would likely fight with the same fanaticism that their predecessors displayed in the Korean War. China has revamped its military forces focusing on cyber and access denial capabilities. Its missile forces, navy and air forces arguably play a more critical role than its ground forces. China is betting on a war that takes place outside its borders, thinking that an enemy force like the United States would be foolhardy to embark on a land invasion of China. The Chinese would seek to destroyUS aircraft carriers with its DF-21D ballistic missile.

What would Pakistan do?

Pakistan is a center of gravity for China's Belt and Road initiative. China has invested many billions of dollars in the construction of the Gwadar Port in Pakistan (and other transport and energy related projects).Gwadar provides "an alternative shipping route to the Malacca Strait, which is frequently patrolled by the United States,"according to the South China Morning Post. Iran is already connected to the Belt and Road via rail. China has helped retool Pakistan's military forces. According to the National Interest, "As Pakistan's relationship has soured with the United States in the past two decades, Pakistan's armed forces have largely looked towards Chinese suppliers for equipment. While China has long supplied Pakistan's armed forces, the relationship has deepened in recent years, with Pakistan making major purchases of top-of-the-line Chinese export equipment." That equipment includes bolstering-Pakistan's nuclear arsenal, fighter aircraft, tanks and short range missiles.

Have to Fight to Get to the Fight

Under Trump, it was clear that American leadership was completely bankrupt. But listening to Blinken and US Secretary of Defense Austin Lloyd, and Biden whine and cry about China and Russia, I can't help but think this is some sort of Hollywood movie sequel from which another sequel is created, and yet another with a slightly different plot and characters, but the same story line.

The reality is that China is not a basket case in any field. Is it realistic and must be understood that China can't afford not to be expansionist. It is a nation with 1.4 billion mouths to feed and a history that dates back to 3,000 years ago. On the other hand, Russia can't afford to be aggressive. With a population of 145 million on a huge landmass that borders 14 countries, it is too risky for Russia to dare to expand globally. President Vladimir Putin knows this well. Under his leadership Russia has become a crafty regional power, moving cautiously (as in Syria) and under cloak and dagger in Ukraine.

The United States would find great difficulty in fighting to get to the fight. Its military forces have not had to face any serious opposition in the air or on the sea during its dismal efforts against guerrilla forces in Afghanistan and Iraq. According to warontherocks.-com:

"China has constructed 72 fighter jet hangars at its three airbases in the Spratlys — Fiery Cross, Mischief, and Subi Reefs — along with another 16 on Woody Island in the Paracels... China has, meanwhile, deployed YJ-12B and YJ-62 antiship cruise missiles to its outposts in the Spratlys and Paracels, backed by longer-range missile capabilities from the mainland. And it has invested heavily in radar and signals intelligence capabilities on all the islands, making it a safe bet that it sees just about anything moving on or above the South China Sea. A US Navy vessel sailing in those waters would be well within the range of Chinese fire when hostilities broke out."

Would the Shanghai Cooperation Organization's (SCO) member and observer states ally with China against the United States? "The Shanghai Cooperation Organization (SCO) is a permanent intergovernmental international organization, the creation of which was announced on 15 June 2001 in Shanghai (China) by the Republic of Kazakhstan, the People's Republic of China, the Kyrgyz Republic, the Russian Federation, the Republic of Tajikistan, and the Republic of Uzbekistan...the SCO counts four observer states, namely the Islamic Republic of Afghanistan, the Republic of Belarus, and the Islamic Republic of Iran, plus the Republic of Mongolia."

Where should the US strike? Gwadar in Pakistan? Chabahar in Iran? The North Korean side of the DMZ? Some SCO countries? How many young Americans would have to die to feed the egos of American political, economic and military leadership and their maniacal quest for full spectrum dominance?

USA Can't Solve its Problems at Home, Needs a Foreign Demon and a War

Plato said democracy leads to anarchy. Is the United States in a transition period to anarchy?

Who knows?

But it is easy to see that former President Trump was a champion of anarchy, of cultural warfare. Just look at the record. Fueled by the fires of the Pandemic of 2020-21over 600,000 people are now dead with the proximate cause of these deaths the hapless federal government that, by Trump's design (Biden proclaimed victory over COVID-19 but a new variant called Delta is beginning to emerge), refused to care for the welfare its citizens; on January 6, 2021, successfully encouraged a mob to take over the US Capitol while congress was in session affirming the electoral college victory of Joe Biden as 46th President of the United States; ignored structural economic, cultural, political and racial owes; allowed Homeland Security shock troops with no identifiable government affiliation picking up protestors on the streets of Portland, Oregon and then dump them into unmarked vans and whisk them away for interrogation; watched as a languished health care system exposed by the COVID19 virus rotted; openly engaged in immigrant bashing; allowed shameful homelessness to fester across the land (includes military veterans and children); and stood idly by as the US

Congress refused to provide a paltry $1200 in financial relief for millions of unemployed citizens torched by not only by the COVID19 virus, but the virus that has become its elected leaders.

And who is the expansionist power here? The United States has 100+ military bases all around the globe. It invaded Iraq, twice. It is still bogged down in Afghanistan with some 18,000 contractors and a few thousand US troops remaining (though now drawing down, the CIA, DIA and mercenaries will still remain in clandestine locations). The USA sends drones to kill terrorists in countries on the African Continent from bases located in friendly countries there. And American soldiers are actively engaged in counternarcotics operations in Colombia.

"Capitalism in the United States is running head on into those problems which impelled Germany in 1914 upon the road of war ... For Germany it was a question of 'organizing' Europe. For the United States it is a question of 'organizing' the world. History is taking mankind directly into the volcanic eruption of American imperialism" said Leon Trotsky.

Chapter 8: The Undead Republican Party Seeks to Overthrow Democracy in America

"With hindsight, it is clear that the United States failed the difficult test set by history. In the three decades that followed their triumph [over the Soviet Union] and their coronation, they proved unable to establish a new world order, to build a role as a parental power or indeed sustain their moral credibility, which is probably lower today than at any time in the last century. Their former adversaries have once more become adversaries, but their former allies no longer truly feel like allies. This moral collapse did not occur overnight; it is the culmination of a long series of blunders, gaffes, setbacks and missteps, under the aegis of a series of presidents whose policies were poles apart."

Amin Maalouf, Adrift: How Our World Lost its Way

"The historic question that must be addressed is: Who is the aberration? Biden and perhaps most of his voters believe that the answer could not be more obvious. It is Trump. But this has been shown to be the wrong answer. The dominant power in the land, the undead Republican Party, has made majority rule aberrant, a notion that transgresses the new norms it has created. From the perspective of this system, it is Biden, and his criminal voters, who are the deviant ones. This is the irony: Trump, the purest of political opportunists, driven only by his own instincts and interests, has entrenched an anti-democratic culture that, unless it is uprooted, will thrive in the long term. It is there in his court appointments, in his creation of a solid minority of at least 45 percent animated by resentment and revenge, but above all in his unabashed demonstration of the relatively unbounded possibilities of an American autocracy."

Fintan O'Toole, Democracy's Afterlife

It gets tiring constantly having to bash on the political, social, military, economic and media leaders in the United States along with fellow citizens of every class and persuasion. But what is a journalist—and citizen—supposed to do when presented with the petulance of a sitting American president in Donald Trump who, defying precedent, refuses to submit to the fact that he lost an election and simply out of spite is placing land mines—in the form of edicts, firings, appointments and executive policy actions— for the incoming president Joe Biden. And what of the Republican party that enables this dangerous precedent?

The American people are currently being crushed by the COVID19 Pandemic (600,000 dead and counting). But here again, a journalist has no choice but to look at anti-maskers and herd immunity pushers and say, What the F*&^? What is it going to take to get Americans to be disciplined, suck it up and do what is necessary to get past this pestilential time both in political and cultural terms?

The United States Congress deserves no better. The American people are suffering physically and economically. Financial assistance is needed from the Federal printing press for states and localities. Taxes have to be raised on some class. Americans have to get off this "no more taxes" kick. How the hell is the United States supposed to fix its infrastructure and medical provisioning system if no one wants to pay for it? Tax a portion of the dividends after a days trading on Wall Street.

Failure is an Option

And what of the failed war in Afghanistan and Iraq? Bring the troops home? Sure, let's do that. But they will just be replaced by Special Operators, contractors who were formerly in the military and assorted paramilitary operatives from the CIA, NSA, and Defense Intelligence Agency. Who wants to give up a great testing ground for new weapons?

What to say about Iraq? Well, nothing much can be said about a puppet regime setup by the United States for the purpose of quelling the protestations of its citizens while the United States using the country as a staging area for a war against Iran.

These are just a handful of the types of "blunders" that Maalouf is referring to and it may, in the near future, cost the United States its democracy.

If leaders can't take care of their people, and citizens fail to hold their representatives to account, then what's the point of waving the American flag and being proud of it. Perhaps the most awful sight to see during the Pandemic of 2020 is the abject failure of the American healthcare system. As Maalouf points out, "The tragedy of 2020 has demonstrated that, if applied to strictly, too blindly, the consequences of Thatcherism [Reaganism, deregulation, privatization] could be monstrous, particularly in the domain of healthcare. Years of savage budget cuts in a sector, that, while not productive is literally vital, led to substantial shortages of staff and medical equipment, and this resulted in a cataclysm that has gravely compromised the moral legitimacy of economic liberalism."

And yet trying to make basic healthcare a "right" in the United States is a Herculean task.

United States Constitution Torn Asunder

Trump and his undead Republican Party are using the time offered by Trump's refusal to concede the presidency to willfully undermine American democracy. Rudy Giuliani and 73 million Trump acolytes —both rich and poor, White, Black and Latino—in the United States are setting the stage for autocratic minority rule; or; less politely, a coup. They are taking a page out of every propaganda campaign used by the United States and other warring nations throughout history: Prior to the start of a war, demonize your opponent and make them less-than-human. It makes it easier to kill and defeat them, to make them enemies.

According to O'Toole:

> "The majority, deficient in both patriotism and sanctity, is unworthy. If it seems to have won, that can only be because, being outside the polity, it has subverted the real polity by fraud. To deny its validity is both patriotic and righteous. Voter suppression, gerrymandering, and the use of the Supreme Court to hand electoral victories to the Republicans are no longer dirty tricks. They are patriotic imperatives. They are not last resorts but first principles. The great comfort of this mentality is that, when the majority can be conjured out of existence, so can the whole idea of defeat. The old norm, whereby the beaten party retreats into a period of reflection and considers why it lost, is gone.

> One half of a two-party system has passed over into a post-democratic state. This reality has to be recognized, and a crucial aspect of that recognition is to accept that the claim Gerald Ford [US President after Richard Nixon resigned] could make in 1974—"Our Constitution works"—no longer applies. After the long national nightmare of Watergate, America could rub its eyes and awaken to a renewed confidence in its system of checks and balances. But the Trump presidency has been no nightmare. It has been daylight delinquency, its transgressions of democratic values on lurid display in all their corruption and cruelty and deadly incompetence.

> There may be much we do not yet know, but what is known (and in most cases openly flaunted) is more than

enough: the Mueller report, the Ukraine scandal, the flagrant self-dealing, the tax evasion, the children stolen from their parents, the encouragement of neo-Nazis, Trump's admission that he deliberately played down the seriousness of the coronavirus. There can be no awakening because the Republicans did not sleep through all of this. They saw it all and let it happen. In electoral terms, moreover, it turns out that they were broadly right. There was no revulsion among the party base. The faithful not only witnessed his behavior, they heard Trump say, repeatedly, that he would not accept the result of the vote. They embraced that authoritarianism with renewed enthusiasm. The assault on democracy now has a genuine, highly engaged, democratic movement behind it."

The Trump Train—and its undead passengers—has left the station and it is going to be a very powerful force in American politics. Trump will play the role he likes best as a powerbroker controlling his many marionettes throughout the land, raising funds, handpicking candidates to run for congress and polluting the airwaves with demagoguery.

Turning the other cheek on this state of affairs is dangerous. President-elect Joe Biden must Exorcise before he can attempt to heal. Yet, he lets the demon run free throughout the land.

CHAPTER 9: LIQUID CAPITALISM: EVERYONE DRINKS IT, SWIMS IN IT, DROWNS IN IT

The most radical socialists; Black Lives Matter (BLM) protesters (Black, White, Latino or Asian); liberal and conservative zealots; diversity and equity gurus; pacifists; denizens of corporates and non-profits; rappers, rockers and country western musicians; Bernie Sanders; racists and White guilt pushers; Baptists, Catholics, and Muslims; children; bland K-16 teachers; members of the military; indeed, every social, cultural, political and economic demographic of the United States of America drinks, swims and drowns in an ocean of Liquid Capitalism. It is nearly as old as humanity itself.

Liquid Capitalism is impressive and horrifying. It floods and absorbs every political movement and message. It dilutes it, repackages it, commodifies it and profits from it. Take the BLM movement. Corporations jumped on the bandwagon finding another bullet point to add to their Multicultural Marketing strategies. BLM is beyond necessary and about time, of course, but look how quickly corporations took up the mantel of political activists: from Coke and Amazon to Walmart and Apple, corporations push the notion that they are really conscientious, nice inclusive people and are going to restructure internally and hire more Blacks from a pool of 13.4 percent of the US population (census.gov figure).

Drowning the Message

Behind the smiling corporate face that supports BLM (and other minority/diversity movements like LGBTQ), lurks the backstabbing bottomline: How to keep Black Identity consumers spending on the products that corporate capitalists produce.

Consider this from Neilson reports:

" When it comes to African-American consumer spending, there are millions, sometimes billions of dollars in revenue at stake," said Andrew McCaskill, Senior Vice President, Global Communications and Multicultural Marketing, Nielsen. "With 43% of the 75 million Millennials in the US identifying as African American, Hispanic or Asian, if a brand doesn't have a multicultural strategy, it doesn't have a growth strategy. The business case for multicultural outreach is clear. African-American consumers, and all diverse consumers, want to see themselves authentically represented in marketing, and they want brands to recognize their value to the bottomline."

And that was in 2017 before the Black Lives Matter movement kicked off. Even BLM has to resort to capitalist practices to keep afloat: The official BLM store is online and needs consumers to purchase clothing and other items to support the movement.

Liquid Capitalism has drowned out the BLM voice. No one in their right mind can't support their cause. But like everything else in the US, their message, as broadcast on television or the WWW, is mixed in with a hundred other product sells and it gets watered down. It is tough to keep those media corporations and their advertisers—who determine what news you'll digest—interested in one subject for too long. News and advertisements—along with Social Justice fare—are repetitively pounded into television viewers heads (and with every click of the user's mouse) and they eventually become numb to what counts. Just as they shrug their shoulders and say, "My gosh, how awful" as another shooting of a Black man is broadcast or a school shooting takes place, they all forget about it in a few weeks time because liquid capitalism dilutes the message by commodifying and selling it for profit, and ultimately it is washed away Besides, there is always a new "thing" just around the corner that will cause an important movement like BLM to drop out of the news cycle.

It's the same story with the Covid-19 pandemic. Here is this gem from a marketing firm (ama.org): "To market to people during this difficult and scary period, to really and cleverly market to them, you must understand their deepest psychological needs. People want what they don't have, and there are ways of figuring out exactly what it is that they don't have and how they'd like it served to them—even during a pandemic."

Liquid Identity

According to Moises Esteban Guitart:

> "Liquid modernity [capitalism] provides an explosion of choices. The number of products or options available has increased dramatically: TV channels, telephonic companies, clothes, varieties of foods, retirement pensions, medical care, different computers, gas services, heterogeneity of families, different kinds of jobs, plurality of religions, and so on. However, several researchers have suggested that materialism, extreme consumption as a way of life, could be toxic to subjective wellbeing The consumerist society fosters individualistic identity and is associated with the creation of infinite needs, hedonistic material pleasure, impulsive and hyperactive behavior, dissatisfaction with the "solid life," craving for novelty, concern with appearance, and deteriorating happiness and interpersonal relations.

> The individualistic liquid identity syndrome is the negative psychological effect of the consumerist capitalism. Individualistic liquid identity is the product of cultural capitalistic tools (concepts like materialism, artifacts like money, and institutions like markets) that people utilize to define and understand themselves and others and they interiorize

explicitly and implicitly. The individualistic liquid identity syndrome affects people that give a high value to money, possessions, autonomy, appearances (physical and social), fame and independence.

The ideologies and institutions of [Liquid] capitalism foster, maintain and encourage a set of values based in materialism, self interest and a selfish, strong desire for financial success and economic growth, hedonism, high levels of consumption and interpersonal styles based on competition. These values and practices often conflict with pursuits such as caring about the broader world, having a close relationships with others, feeling worthy and free, and sharing or solidarity."

Corporations Say, "A Tribal Nation is More Profitable than a Unified Nation"

Liquid Capitalism is destroying the fabric of the United States. Businesses go where the cash is whether it is an LGBTQ Identity market ($3.7 trillion spending power says apple.com) or Latino Identity market ($1.7 trillion according to forbes.com). Corporations and their politicians in the US Congress are salivating for a time when the USA consists of many Identity Tribes. And they are using artificial intelligence according to federalist.com to accelerate that process.

"When we identify ourselves and allow ourselves to be identified, when we tribe up and proclaim the characteristics that are uniform throughout our tribe, we give advertisers and marketers just what they've been looking for all these years: groups of conformed individuals to whom they can sell things. The last century proved to marketers and advertisers that they could create products that were geared to be consumed by specific subsets of the population, from fan bases to ethnic groups. The new way to do this is through AI and machine learning algorithms that do more than target individuals who subscribe to group identities—it actually herds us into identities…Advertisers are specifically targeting individuals based on their revealed group identity, and the algorithms that are being designed to help us, to give us the content we want, are driving our choices as much as (if not more than) we are driving them."

Great! Now Artificial Intelligence and Machine Language is in on the gig.

The fact is there is no escape from Liquid Capitalism. Even leading advocates of Equity in Education/Social Justice are bound by the dictates of capitalism. Take the case of Australia. It has followed US federal, state and local schemes that push the privatization of education. Here in the US, as in Australia, "Schools compete against each other via test scores; public schools are required to fight for limited resources and for the most talented teachers and students; competition [capitalism] has been significantly amplified by the publication of student performance data; competition includes the creation of unforgiving performance cultures, which result in teachers spending more time "working for the numbers" than delivering pastoral care or addressing issues of equity and inclusion; and young people are sandwiched, therefore, into the same cookie-cutter model of excellence that schools must adopt to retain market competitiveness."

Note: I have witnessed first hand "working for the numbers" in a public middle school. Students in a virtual class were given A's across the board even though some did not complete an assignment work or only partially did so. One teacher quipped, "We've got to keep them coming back, right?"

Eliminate False Consciousness? Reeducation

There is no question that Equity in Education and Social Justice require an alteration of American language/thought. This is commonly called Inclusive Language. Who isn't for that, if it is implemented sensibly?

To get there, the US public and private school systems have become the primary targets of education strategies pushed by Equity/Inclusion and Social Justice Missionaries (capitalists), regulators and politicians, (lobbied by capitalists) and; of course, corporations. Beyond the noble cause they all proclaim, they all have a financial interest, or capitalist incentive, even as they seek to challenge the norms of American education and language that are insensitive to all minority groups. Get em while they are young, as the saying goes.

American educators, with the "Change" Missionaries in the vanguard, claim that they will transform the inequitable language and thought processes used by some 328 million Americans (they are sure to make a lot of money in the process). But to what end, all this? To some advocates, the goal seems to be to lead the charge to force the majority population to acknowledge its sin of "Whiteness and inherent bias" and "White Violence" that has limited minority freedom of movement in American society whether in the athletic, economic, political or cultural spheres. To other advocates it means fighting to maintain LGBTQ rights, or pushing against ageism, and ensuring societal inclusiveness for those with disabilities (to include military veterans). And to others it is remembering the past pernicious segregation of Mexican Americans in Arizona schools.

To put a fine point on it all, all Americans are being subjected to a massive reeducation campaign. It is also mandate from corporate and military America. It'll work as long as the practice of shaming by some advocates or particular portion of the American populace is removed.

And the flow of Liquid Capitalism makes it all happen.

Corporations and the US military are well into the process of the reeducation effort. Consider Goldman Sachs manual for Inclusive Language. In it, employees are instructed in the proper use of pronouns. "Goldman Sachs has launched an internal campaign centered on gender identity and pronouns, seeking to provide education on what the different types of pronouns are, guidance for the way to use them and offering new avenues for our people to proactively self-identify."

Over at Lockheed Martin an ALL-INclusive campaign has been underway since 2019: Transforming for Impact program is well underway: "We define inclusion as acknowledging and leveraging diversity by creating an environment where employees feel welcomed, respected, engaged and able to bring their full self to work in order to develop innovative solutions that drive business success."

Then there is the US Army's Project Inclusion: "The Army has enacted a range of initiatives, to include training. The training helps to increase deliberate thinking and shift attention from the visual construct and keep the focus on the value that diversity brings… [we are] redacting race, ethnicity, and gender data from both the Officer and Enlisted Record Briefs."

Original Sins

In the end, the human species is Capitalist to the core. Archeological finds from the city of Uruk in southern Mesopotamia (4000 to 3100 BC) show that some of the first writings in human history were used to document expenses and revenues for "transactions involving grain and sheep." Independently, Egypt (Old Kingdom 2700-2200 BC) developed its own writing system and used it for similar purposes. If that were not Capitalist enough, trade in obsidian (volcanic black glass used to make tools and weapons) between Bingol in Eastern Anatolia to sites hundreds of kilometers away in Mesopotamia and the Levant took place in 10,000 (BC) by river and overland routes (see Making Civilizations: The World before 600, Harvard, 2020).

And humanity's original sins of war, slavery and Capitalism are at least that old. Will we ever rid ourselves of them?

CHAPTER 10: LIFE DURING A TRUMP SECOND TERM (AND A BIDEN PRESIDENCY?): PARA-MILITARY DEMOCRACY ACCELERATES

"We must take sides. Neutrality helps the oppressor, never the victim. Silence encourages the tormentor, never the tormented. Sometimes we must interfere. When human lives are endangered, when human dignity is in jeopardy, national borders and sensitivities become irrelevant. Wherever men and women are persecuted because of their race, religion, or political views, that place must —at that moment—become the center of the universe."

Ellie Weisel, The Night Trilogy

"In November, Black Girls Ride will rev our engines, we will go to the polls and fill the ballot boxes of this nation and choose a leader that will provide the unity our country needs. We invite you to vote like your life depends on it. Thank you."

Porsche Taylor, Black Girls Ride at the Get Off Ours Necks rally in Washington, DC.

Two Headed Monster: One Side is Out of Control and Who Knows About the Other?

Sides must be taken.

Americans must choose the side of the Kenosha, Wisconsin protestors and the two men killed by a teenage YMCA lifeguard and supporter of President Donald Trump. Trump must be soundly defeated on November 3, 2020. He is America's Mussolini and his followers the equivalent of Mussolini's followers the Black Shirts.

The American election process only produces two candidates for presidential office. For the foreseeable future, Americans are stuck with a system dominated by Republicans and Democrats, awash in large donor money and polluted by Political Action Committees. Talk of imposing term limits, eliminating the Electoral College, instituting referenda, and developing robust third parties are just that: talk. Americans are too lazy to be revolutionaries for change which is one of the many reasons cookie-cutter candidates from both political parties make the grade as presidential timber.

Indeed, Americans are represented by a two-headed monster and it is difficult to divine the difference between the two parties. But one head of that monster, the Republican ghoul in the guise of Donald Trump, has gone off the rails. It is trying to rip itself away from the Janus-faced Democratic side of its body and intends to reconstitute itself as a singular sort of Republican Lotan not only of the sea but adapted to the land. The Republican party has become home to racists, fascists, militant cops, Q'Non, the Boogaloo Boys, a rag tag army of right wing militias, and corporate vampires who want to pay no taxes, privatize Social Security, and rule over a wasteland of unemployed and homeless Americans. In short, it is the Republican party is the party of ignorance and oppression.

Joe Biden, a kind of conservative, not quite an elderly Yoda, called from exile on Planet Delaware, is no Ha'dad Ba'al to Lotan, but a vote for Biden represents a hold-the-line measure until a Ha'dad Ba'al arrives in some form to purge the United States of the social and environmental diseases that Trump and the Republicans have exacerbated over the past four years (with complicity of many Democrats).

Yes, Biden's fatherly advice was absent when it came to Hunter Biden; the nefarious "yes" vote for the second Iraq War; his support for the 1994 Crime Bill (although there is a lot of fog around some of the facts on the matter); and his Wall Street ties leads to a grimace. Further, Biden seems to be "playing not to lose" which is a dangerous strategy. "Protecting the lead" by going conservative is not a smart play.

UPDATE: In June of 2021 the US Treasury began moving $350 billion in Pandemic relief funds states, local and tribal communities. According to Newsweek, Biden urged leaders at the three levels to push much of the funds to police departments and other policing-related organizations in the USA. He also is backing away from raising taxes on the wealthy to pay for infrastructure programs. The BBC reports that there are more than 2,000 children being held in a tent city at a military base in the state of Texas known as Fort Bliss. The conditions there, they report, are appalling with lice infestation, disease and filthy facilities. Yes, Joe Biden, you are now the commander in chief of your very own Gulag.

So what's an American citizen supposed to do? Not vote and proclaim to friends and family that the candidates are beneath one's dignity and, well, "I can't morally cast my vote for x or y." Or, "Oh me, oh my, it's the lesser of two evils and I voted for y instead of x. I held my nose even." Bull*&^%!

The importance of the 2020 election can be found in the impassioned, and convincing, speeches from the Get Off My Neck March. There really is only one sane choice.

Trump (and Biden?) Dystopia: Paramilitary Democracy

During a Trump second term, the militarization of the United States will accelerate (we are seeing this under Biden too). National Guard and active duty military personnel will occupy urban spaces which will become the site of relentless anti-Trump and pro-Black Lives Matter protesters.

- Increased violence between right and left wing groups across the United States will be the norm. Left wing groups will arm themselves forming counter-militias of their own. Gun battles will take place between the two opposing groups during nationwide protests against a Trump reelection. Police will be overwhelmed as they will not be able to quell riots, stop gun battles or perform routine policing duties. A wild card will be urban gangs. What alliances will they make? The active duty military will have to intervene.

- Austerity measures to pay the bill for the COVID19 Pandemic relief will be put into force. Unemployment and homelessness will explode. Work camps will need to be setup to deal with the needy masses. Chain-gang style employment, without the chains, will be initiated to work on infrastructure projects. Defense contractors and prison industries will make millions as they oversee work camps and provide security.

- Mutated COVID19, mixed with seasonal flu strains, will flow throughout the United States causing increased infections and death. Trump and his minions will encourage this development because it will clear the system of minorities, the elderly and the infirm.

- The US healthcare system will drown in a new wave of COVID Delta cases. States and localities will go bankrupt because they will not receive financial assistance or proper supplies. Americans will still scoff at the idea of paying more taxes to fight the Pandemic. Death rates for other diseases (cancer, heart disease, etc.) will soar as non-COVID19 patients with those conditions will be turned away from care. Insurance companies will go broke paying on policies. The infected will be sent to and imprisoned in unused athletic stadiums. The military will be used to herd the sick into holding pens and secure them there.

- Right-wing, fascist Boogaloo Boys and Q'Non will continue to designate as Republican, run for political office, and, once elected, begin to infiltrate local, state and federal representative bodies.

- Trump will take the nation to war against Iran (if not Biden). Israel, Saudi Arabia and the UAE will be allies, even as American business in Afghanistan, Iraq and Syria has not been concluded: US troops still remain active in these countries. It is likely the United States would have to draft its young people to fight such a war. Anti-American violence will explode in Afghanistan, Iraq, Syria, Lebanon, Turkey, and scores of other countries around the globe.

- Environmental regulations, species protections will be eliminated.

- "[America's] atrocious record with regard to the human rights of its citizens suggests that, with parliamentary complicity, it is degenerating to the status of a paramilitary democracy." The United States will continue to slide to becoming a degenerate military state.

- Under relentless attack by Trump and his stooges, the First Amendment will be shattered (we will see what Biden does). Media will become further centralized. Americans will be fed larger doses disinformation. Alternative media sites will come under threat of removal if they incur the wrath of Trump & Friends. Thus:

> "Hazards of centralized mass media include the following: 1.) A disproportion of power occurs and disproportionate informational power accrues to those who control centralized mass media; arguably, it is inherently undemocratic. 2.) An inability to transmit tacit knowledge; the context of

content presented must either be explicitly explained or is assumed to be understood by the receiver. 3.) An inclination to focus on the unusual and sensational to capture the receivers' attention, leading to a distortion and trivialization of reality. 4.) The deliberate promotion of emotions such as anxiety, fear, or greed can be used to sell a particular agenda. 5.) An inability to deal with complex issues because of time and economic constraints leads to simplification, further distorting and trivializing reality." US Army Special Forces Manual, 2008

CHAPTER 11: Snake Plissken for President in 2020! No Donald "Erdogan" Trump! No Joe "Empath" Biden!

Bob Hauk: There was an accident. About an hour ago, a small jet went down inside New York City. The President was on board.
Snake Plissken: President of what?
Bob Hauk: That's not funny, Plissken. You go in, find the President, bring him out in 24 hours, and you're a free man.
Snake Plissken: 24 hours, huh?
Bob Hauk: I'm making you an offer.
Snake Plissken: Bull&%$#!
Bob Hauk: Straight just like I said.
Snake Plissken: I'll think about it.
Bob Hauk: No time. Give me an answer.
Snake Plissken: Get a new president!
Bob Hauk: We're still at war, Plissken. We need him alive.
Snake Plissken: I don't give a f*&^ about your war. . .or your president.
Bob Hauk: Is that your answer?

Escape from New York, 1981 (movie)

In the dark, comedy-drama science fiction cult classic Escape from New York, New York City (the Manhattan borough but referred to here as New York City) has become a penitentiary secured by "50 foot high concrete walls and the bridges are all mined." Aircraft that patrol its perimeter fire on and kill any prisoners who scale the wall and make it near the top.

If President Donald Trump wins a second term, he probably will attempt to build a wall on the northern border and continue his southern border barrier project. He will issue subsequent orders for patrolling drones to shoot and kill anyone trying to get in or out. He'll have a mandate to do it after a 2020 election victory and will have an obsequious military to carry out the building of and security for such a wall. Large American urban centers will teem with paramilitary enforcers of Trump's elected dictatorship.

Anyway, the Supermax New York City prison in Escape from New York was needed because the United States had turned into one massive crime scene from border to border. There was a 400 percent increase in crime. New York City, with massive buildings in place, surrounded by water, was an ideal place for a prison to house the worst criminals in the United States.

One can't but help watch the cast of characters who play the movie's characters without some admiration. They include Kurt Russell (SD Snake Plissken), Lee Van Cleef (Hauk, Commissioner US Police Force), Donald Pleasence (President), Ernest Borgnine (Cabbie, jazz fanatic), Isaac Hayes (the Duke), Adrienne Barbeau (Maggie), and Harry Dean Stanton (Brain).

John Carpenter co-wrote and directed Escape from New York. In a You Tube interview he said that he "wrote the screenplay in the mid-1970's during the time of Watergate when Nixon was run out of office because he was involved in a burglary. The whole feeling in the nation was of real cynicism about our president…Its kind of America in a way, put into the future. It's…our fears."

After a long and deadly trek, Snake succeeds in getting the president out of New York City. The rescue was made more urgent by a cassette tape of a speech on nuclear fusion that the president was carrying. The tape's contents would lead to the end of the war that the US was waging against China and the Soviet Union (Russia).

The president, as played by Donald Pleasence, is a close approximation of Donald Trump; or, arguably, any president. When the president's Air Force One is falling from the sky, his words to the doomed crew are, "God save me and watch over you." Pleasence's president is smarmy and psychopathic. After Snake has gotten the president to safety he asks for a few minutes of the president's time. Here is the dialogue that follows:

President: I want to thank you back there for saving my life. If there's anything you want... anything at all...
Snake Plissken: Just a moment of your time.
President: Of course…Yes?
Snake Plissken: We did get you out. But a lot of people died in the process. I just wondered how you felt about it.
President: Well, I...I wanna thank them. This nation appreciates their sacrifice."

The president leaves Snake and moves to a microphone to play the contents of the tape. He fetches the tape from his briefcase not knowing that Snake replaced the president's tape with Cabbie's jazz tape. The president loads what he thinks is a recording dealing with nuclear fusion into a tape-deck and what gets aired is Cabbie's Bandstand Boogie. Snake walks away while pulling the tape out of the president's cassette and ripping it up.

Why Snake for President of the United States?

Snake is a decorated combat veteran, a plus for any presidential candidate. He gets the job done: the buck stops with him. Americans like a clean beginning and end, not an endless War on Terror. He'd have acted on the COVID 19 Pandemic aggressively.

Plissken speaks his mind, pulls no punches. He is a big believer in the First Amendment to the US Constitution.

Snake is a firearms/weapons specialist. He supports the Second Amendment.

He has a wry sense of humor. He knows the world needs to lighten up. He knows Jazz is good medicine for an uptight world.

Snake is an Independent. He has not been vetted by the Democratic or Republican Party. He owes nothing to them.

Snake works with the downtrodden, the imprisoned. He is a diversity candidate.

He had enough of the American federal government and war. He knew the process that manufactures US presidents is absolutely corrupt.

Snake was imprisoned for robbing a bank. He'd be no fan of the police, Wall Street or big banking concerns.

A Donald "Erdogan" Trump Second Term

Trump is taking a page out of Recep Erdogan's, president of Turkey, electoral playbook. If Trump scores a second term as president the media analysis will read exactly like this 2018 report from Haaretz:

"In elections that were neither free nor fair, President Recep Tayyip Erdogan stage-managed a mandate for ultimate power…But the victory is at expense of national cohesion. The country is more divided than ever - while looking ahead towards an economic disaster… The June 2018 elections will go down as the day that Turkey's opposition could have defeated President Recep Tayyip Erdogan and halted the country's decent towards an elected dictatorship, but failed…There's also of course the fact that the elections were neither free nor fair. Erdogan and the AKP used state resources to ensure victory. The media is almost totally pro-Erdogan after years of co-option and censorship. On election day, there were reported cases of fraud, including ballot stuffing, an incident where a car filled with ballots was pulled over heading to a polling station near the southern city of Urfa. Ahead of the elections, legislation was passed to allow ballots without official seals to be counted…"

A Joe "Empath" Biden Victory

As a reminder of Joe Biden's "empathy" we turn to a piece written in The Guardian in 2019.

"As times have changed, Biden has expressed retrospective misgivings about some of those earlier actions and stances. For example, he very recently attempted to offer an apology of sorts, more like an un-apology, to Anita Hill, which she quite understandably rejected. And he remains a pure, dyed-in-the-wool neoliberal, as much as ever a tool of Wall Street and corporations. We deserve better than a candidate who wants us to look past his record and focus only on the image he wants to project and, when that tack fails, can offer progressives only a "my bad".

[Biden's] most conspicuous affront to women was his role as chair of the Senate judiciary committee in condoning committee members' vile and viciously sexist attacks on Anita Hill when she came forward to testify against the supreme court nominee Clarence Thomas. He then abruptly adjourned the hearing while two other female former employees of the Equal Employment Opportunity Commission under Thomas were waiting to give testimony corroborating Hill's allegations; Biden thus assured confirmation of one of the worst, most dangerously conservative supreme court appointees of the 20th century.

In addition to Biden's disturbing record on domestic policy, he has been a consistent warmonger. He has supported every military intervention he's been able to, including, most disastrously voting for the 2002 resolution authorizing war against Iraq and ushering the country into the endless war against "terror" we remain immersed in."

The movie it's Mad, Mad, Mad, Mad World comes to mind.

Chapter 12: US National Security Strategy is Meant to Protect Wall Street, Congress, the White House, and the Pentagon

"Our fundamental responsibility is to protect the American people, the homeland, and the American way of life."

– National Security Strategy of the United States, 2017 (President Donald Trump)

"The United States government has no greater responsibility than protecting the American people."

– National Security Strategy, 2015 (President Barack Obama)

"At home our most important priority is to protect the homeland for the American people."

– The National Security Strategy of the United States of Americas, 2002 (President George W. Bush)

The United States' National Security Strategy is based on foundational Instruments of National Power (INP). The INP consists of Diplomacy, Informational, Military, Economic, Financial, Law Enforcement, Information. Combined with the INP's support, they combine to protect an economy and society that has an annual Gross Domestic Product of nearly $20 trillion (USD) and a per capita income of almost $60 thousand according to the CIA's World Fact Book. In that publication, the CIA notes that "US firms are at or near the forefront in technological advances, especially in computers, pharmaceuticals, and medical, aerospace, and military equipment…"

This incredible wealth and power, and the mythical status of America's technologies, could not stop three disastrous events; two of which could have been prevented (911 and great recession), and the third mitigated (COVID-19).

Over the last 19 years, the American people have been exposed to a deadly virus (COVID-19), a brutal economic recession in 2008, and terrorist attacks in 2001 on two symbols of American power. And in each case, the response of the US government was to first pump trillions of dollars into Wall Street's coffers through bailouts and quantitative easing, while, in comparison, main street got billions of pennies tossed their way.

The national security strategies pushed out by three American presidents (two Republicans and one Democrat) claim the number one priority of the US government is to protect the American people. But as the three shock and awe events of the last 19 years demonstrate, the American people that are protected by the national security strategy are the wealthy and powerful classes and institutions that run the country from their perches on Wall Street, in the White House and Congress, and the Pentagon.

The middle and lower class workers are an afterthought.

Wall Street Mafia

Wall Street is, in fact, a threat to the country. Its focus on increasing return on investment for shareholders has crippled investment in the real economy (infrastructure, retooling, etc.). A better description of Wall Street would be the Wall Street Mafia. An extortion racket if there ever was one. Consider Harvard Business Review's, The Price of Wall Street's Power:

"Scholars and executives alike have criticized Wall Street not only for promoting short-term thinking but for sacrificing the interests of employees and customers to benefit shareholders and for encouraging dishonesty from executives who feel they're being asked to meet impossible demands. The financial sector's influence on management has become so powerful that a recent survey of chief financial officers showed that 78% would "give up economic value" and 55% would cancel a project with a positive net present value—that is, willingly harm their companies—to meet Wall Street's targets and fulfill its desire for "smooth" earnings.

Executives often explain their deference to Wall Street by saying they have a "fiduciary duty" to maximize shareholder returns. That's been an article of faith since 1970, when Milton Friedman wrote in the New York Times that executives' only responsibility was maximizing profits. The problem, however, is that it's not true. Whatever your beliefs about the moral responsibilities of executives, a fiduciary duty is a specific legal obligation, and law professor Lynn Stout has shown that as a matter of law American executives simply do not face any such requirement.

From 1998 through 2013 the finance, insurance, and real estate industries spent almost $6 billion on lobbying; the only sector to spend more was health care. In the wake of the 2008 crisis, the financial sector actually intensified its pressure on the government. Look at the 2013–2014 election cycle: As of March 2014 finance, insurance, and real estate had spent almost $485 million on lobbying—more than any other industry—and had donated almost $149 million to the campaigns of federal candidates, nearly three times as much as health care had donated.

Representatives and lobbyists of the financial sector are so entwined with the agencies that are supposed to regulate it that Washingtonians collectively refer to them as " The Blob." This is reflected in the résumés of current and former government officials.

The White House and Congress: Self-Quarantine for 10 Years, Please

President Trump's la-dee-da attitude during the initial spread of COVID-19 should have come as no surprise. A virus himself, Trump's preference would probably have been to let COVID-19 cull the human herd by not instituting mass testing of the American populace. A dark reading of that thinking being that people infected would continue to travel around the United States passing along COVID-19 to others.

Vox reported that:

"Politico reporter Dan Diamond told NPR [National Public Radio] host Terry Gross that, based on his own reporting, Trump "did not push to do aggressive additional testing in recent weeks, and that's partly because more testing might have led to more cases being discovered of coronavirus outbreak, and the president had made clear — the lower the numbers on coronavirus, the better for the president, the better for his potential re-election this fall."

Trump's response to the COVID-19 pandemic brings to mind a scene in the movie classic Total Recall (1990 version) where the sinister character Victor Cohagen (played by Ronnie Cox) is told by an engineer that if he cuts off oxygen supply to one of the city sectors, inhabitants there will die.

Cohagen: Yes, what is it?
Underling: Sir, the oxygen level is bottoming out in sector G –
what do you want me to do about it?
Cohagen: Don't do anything.
Underling: But they won't last an hour sir.
Cohagen: Fuck 'em.

In the US senate, conservative ideology takes precedent over the suffering of the American people. The plebes are being slow-rolled. According to USA Today "Sen. Lamar Alexander, R-Tenn., who chairs the Health, Education, Labor and Pensions Committee, objected to fast-tracking the legislation. He acknowledged workers are struggling but said businesses are also struggling and that an expensive federal mandate wouldn't help them."

The general public might have the impression that the US government had no plan of action for the invasion of the COVID-19 organism. In 2006, President George W. Bush laid down a template for dealing with a pandemic that should have been implemented as China (fast forward to 2020), and subsequently, the rest of the world, coped with the spread of COVID-19. Though the Bush strategy was focused on influenza, all the core steps the US government had to take immediately were well articulated.

"The Strategy provides a high-level overview of the approach that the Federal Government will take to prepare for and respond to a pandemic, and articulates expectations of non-Federal entities to prepare themselves and their communities. The Strategy contains three pillars: (1) preparedness and communication; (2) surveillance and detection; and (3) response and containment. Preparedness for a pandemic requires the establishment of infrastructure and capacity, a process that can take years. For this reason, significant steps must be taken now. The Strategy affirms that the Federal Government will use all instruments of national power to address the pandemic threat.

Up, Up and Away, in My Beautiful Military-Intelligence Balloon

The combined US National Security budget (uniform services, contractors, nuclear weapons development at the Department of Energy, operations, etc.) is roughly $1.25 trillion per year, according to an analysis by the Project for Government Oversight (POGO) and the Center for Defense Information conducted in 2019.

That is a staggering $1.25 trillion in 2019 and you can bet that going forward that yearly figure is likely to rise. It is the White House and US Congress that sign off on that amount year after year.

"Our final annual tally for war, preparations for war, and the impact of war comes to more than $1.25 trillion—more than double the Pentagon's base budget. If the average taxpayer were aware that this amount was being spent in the name of national defense—with much of it wasted, misguided, or simply counterproductive—it might be far harder for the national security state to consume ever-growing sums with minimal public pushback. For now, however, the gravy train is running full speed ahead and its main beneficiaries—Lockheed Martin, Boeing, Northrop Grumman, and their cohorts—are laughing all the way to the bank."

And what about the costs for wars on terror, Iraq, Syria and Afghanistan and its effects on America's economy?

According to the publication The Balance :

"The War on Terror is a military campaign launched by President George W. Bush in response to the al-Qaida 9/11 terrorist attacks. The War on Terror includes the Afghanistan War and the War in Iraq. It added $2.4 trillion to the debt as of the FY 2020 budget.

The War in Afghanistan has lasted longer than the Vietnam War. The War in Iraq killed 4,419 US soldiers and wounded 31,994 more.59 Taxpayers have spent more than $1.52 trillion on the wars in Afghanistan, Iraq, and Syria.

The real cost of the War on Terror is not just what it has added to the debt. It's also the lost jobs that those funds could have created. By some estimates, every $1 billion spent on defense creates 8,555 jobs and adds $565 million to the economy.61 That same $1 billion given to you as a tax cut would have stimulated enough demand to create 10,779 jobs and put $505 million into the economy as retail spending. And $1 billion in education spending adds $1.3 billion to the economy and creates 17,687 jobs.

Using this model, the $2.4 trillion spent on the War on Terror created 20 million jobs and added $1.4 trillion to the economy. But if it had gone toward education instead, it would have created almost 42 million jobs. It would have added $3.1 trillion to the economy. That may have helped end the recession sooner."

Trump's Stimulus Package

Trump has proposed about $850 billion in economic stimulus (in addition to the billions in the House of Representatives aid package lingering in the Senate). So that's a one time shot of about $1 trillion for America's suffering plebeians.

Sounds good until you realize that one of Trump's proposals in his stimulus package is to suspend the payroll tax which funds Social Security. Even in the face of a national health and economic emergency, opportunistic Trump seeks to cripple Social Security.

According to the Motley Fool,

"Social Security collected more than $885 billion in payroll tax contributions in 2018, the most recent year for which the Social Security trustees have made information available. That represented the vast majority of the roughly $1 trillion in revenue that Social Security received, and it was enough to pay almost 90% of all the benefits that Social Security recipients got that year.If Social Security stopped receiving that $885 billion, the impact would be immediate. Benefits would have to get funded almost entirely by trust fund balances. With asset levels of about $2.9 trillion, the program could only go for four years before using up its entire savings. Even if a payroll tax cut lasted only for the last nine months of

2020, the roughly $660 billion hit would dramatically accelerate the time at which the trust funds would be empty."

In 1972, President Richard Nixon compared the average American to a young child in a family. Nothing has changed in 2020. Wall Street, the White House, the US Congress and the Pentagon treat the American people as children.

The lyrics to Woody Guthrie's song, This Land is Your Land ring true in 2020 just as they did in the original version in 1940:

As I went walking, I saw a sign there,
And on the sign there, it said "Private Property."
But on the other side, it didn't say nothing!
That side was made for you and me.
In the squares of the city, in the shadow of a steeple,
By the relief office, I'd seen my people.
As they stood there hungry, I stood there asking,
Is this land made for you and me?

Chapter 13: Two Face America—73 Million Trump Party Apparatchiks Guarantee Turmoil Over the Coming Years

It is happening here.

The soul of America is like the character Two Face in the Batman movie series.

One defeat of the Party of Trump and its 73 million apparatchiks is not enough. In Trump, the United States has bred its own dictator in waiting and he's got an army of servile apostles willing to fight and die for him. Vigilance by his opponents has never been more important.

"This Fuhrer dictatorship could produce only lackeys and profiteers of the most reactionary and aggressive part of German imperialist reaction. Its Germanic democracy reared the repulsive type of a human breed that was boundlessly servile to men of higher rank and just as boundlessly cruelly tyrannical towards men below it," Georg Lukacs writing in The Destruction of Reason.

Incumbent (now former) President Donald Trump now owns the Republican Party, lock, stock and barrel. With 73 million restless apparatchiks clearly beholden to the cult of Trump, will it be long before the Republican Party gets rebranded as the Trump National Party; or, perhaps, the MAGA Party (Make America Great Again)? Maybe Trump sells-off his faltering real estate empire and creates a media conglomerate—consisting of television, radio,and the Internet/WWW—that spews out divisive, fascist, ultraconservative fare 24 hours a day, 7 days week. Trump Media would absorb the National Review, New York Post and similar conservative publications/websites.

Sky's the limit for Trump: His 73 million followers include an increasing number of Blacks and Latinos who appear to revere him for his apparent strength, tough talk and sense of honor.

According to Fortune Magazine, "As Trump once put it: 'Real power is fear. It's all about strength. Never show weakness. You've always got to be strong. Don't be bullied. There is no choice.'"

Adolf Hitler Said That Too

"Brutality is respected. The ordinary man in the street only respects brute force and ruthlessness. The people need to be kept in a salutary state of fear. They want to fear something. Why make a fuss over brutality and wax indignant over tortures? The masses want ti. They want something that will give them shudders of terror. Moralistic platitudes are essential for the masses. There could be no greater mistake for a politician than to be seen posing as the immoral superman. Of course I shall not make it a matter of principle whether or not to act immorally in the conventional sense. I do not abide, you see, by any principles whatever." (Adolf Hitler quoted in The Destruction of Reason by Georg Lukacs)

We are all familiar with these wicked sentiments expressed by Trump and Hitler and assorted cult leaders, or should be. The history books are replete with tales of dastardly kings, princes and dictators who said nearly the same things and lived and ruled by such dictates. Democracy has been the aberration in politics, not dictatorship or kingship.

The Path to an American Hitler

The Destruction of Reason by Lukacs traces the development of irrationalism and fascism in Germany; specifically, the intellectual fertilizer that led to Hitler's rise to power and National Socialism. His analysis reaches back to 1789 and includes commentary on

Hegel, Kant, Nietzsche, Marx, Engels, and scores of other philosophical heavyweights.

In an epilogue to the book titled Post World War II Irrationalism, Lukacs argues that the USA achieved all that Hitler sought without all the baggage of National Socialism, psychopathic leaders and the industrialized murder of the Jewish people.

He kicks off the epilogue by quoting from Norman Mailer's novel The Naked and the Dead, specifically the character of General Cummings:

> "As kinetic energy, a country is organization, coordinated effort, your epithet, fascism. Historically the purpose of this war is to translate America's potential into kinetic energy. The concept of fascism, far sounder that communism, if you consider it, for it is grounded firmly in men's actual natures, merely started in the wrong country, in a country that did not have enough intrinsic potential power to develop completely. In Germany with that basic frustration of limited physical means there were bound to be excesses. But the dreams, the concept was sound enough. For the past century the entire historical process has been working toward greater and greater consolidation of power."

Lukacs ruminates on the United States succeeding as a fascist state where Hitler could not:

> "In contrast to [Nazi] Germany, the USA had a constitution which was democratic from the start. The ruling class managed, particularly during the imperialist era, to have the democratic forms so effectively preserved that by democratically legal means, it achieved a dictatorship of monopoly capitalism at lest as firm as that which Hitler set up with tyrannical procedures. This smoothly functioning

democracy, so called, was created by the Presidential prerogative, the Supreme Court's authority in constitutional questions (and the monopoly capitalists always decided which were the constitutional questions), the finance monopoly over the press, radio, etc., electioneering costs, which successfully prevented really democratic parties from springing up besides the two parties of monopoly capitalism, and lastly the use of terrorist devices (the lynching system—targeting Blacks). And this democracy could in substance realize everything sought by Hitler without needing to break with democracy formally."

Lukacs also notes in passing that Hitler was a fan of American advertising and used what he learned from that field to ply his destructive trade in Germany and across Europe.

Lost Souls

Now we turn to Trita Parsi the Executive Vice President of the Quincy Institute discussing the tortured soul of America:

"If Joe Biden was right and the 2020 presidential elections were a contest over the soul of America, then his victory is bittersweet. With almost half of the votes cast for Donald Trump, he is undeniably very much a part of the American soul…Trump is not an aberration, but a reflection of the ugliness that very much is, and always has been, a part of us. While the US may not yet be ready to grapple with this reality, the rest of the world can no longer afford to live in denial. Around the world, many hoped that the lies we have told ourselves of our American innocence – the lies that form the bedrock of American Exceptionalism and neatly separate us from the desperate impulses that brought forward Trump – would prove true. They didn't.

Almost eight million more Americans voted for Trump this past Tuesday than they did in 2016. They saw the divisions he fueled, the xenophobia he embraced, the children he caged, the white supremacists he refused to condemn, and the pandemic he bungled; and they weighed that against the tax cuts they won, the conservative Supreme Court judges he appointed, the climate chaos they can ignore, and the punishments he inflicted on the "liberal elites". They decided they wanted four more years of Trump."

As the legendary American actress Betty Davis once said in character, "Fasten your seat belts, it's going to be a bumpy night."